SACRED INNER DIALOGUE

(SID)

Ataana Badilli

SACRED INNER DIALOGUE (SID)
Ataana Badilli

Print ISBN: 978-1-48359-519-1
eBook ISBN: 978-1-48359-520-7

TABLE OF CONTENTS

ATAANA BADILLI

At an early age, Ataana experienced an awakening that made him aware of God's presence and the Oneness in all of existence. He knew that he would assist others in their awakening process and healing journey. Ataana immersed himself in studying and learning about healing, world religions, shamanism, spirituality, psychology and everything related to the mind, body, soul and the mysteries of existence. Ataana awoke to deep inner visions that allowed him to see and understand future and present projections based on energy flow and everything and everyone around him. He also understood complex multi-dimensional patterns, karma, and morphogenetic fields.

He gained access to the Oneness and Multidimensionality of realities. It was perfectly normal for Ataana to see past and parallel lives. It was also intrinsic for him to intuitively apply transformational energy when required. The deep mysteries of life fascinated and guided Ataana in a way that he became a mystic himself, and he soon combined his spiritual insights with learned knowledge. The definition for a mystic describes Ataana's journey substantially: a person who seeks by contemplation and self-surrendering to obtain unity with the absolute.

At the age of twenty, God's energy was amplified in and around Ataana for seven days. Feeling this powerful presence, Ataana decided to devote his life to healing work and to become a teacher and healer. On his ensuing journey, he experienced suffering, unhealthy patterns, addictions, human trauma, feeling disconnected from source, dysfunctional behaviors, the beauty of friendship, life, love, and the quest and realization of Enlightenment. A profound purification process at the age of twenty-seven led him to embark on formal studies in natural medicine. Ataana attended Naturopathic schools in Berlin and Cologne, Germany, and was later initiated into Shamanism and other healing modalities. From then on, Ataana supported healing and transformation wherever he traveled and volunteered his services until he became a spiritual teacher.

At the core of Ataana's teachings, it is comprised of encouraging the rise of consciousness and living up to our fullest potential. Energy and transformational work allow us to remember how to live in balance with all of creation. Ataana inspires us to tune in, activate and access all of our energy to unveil our highest and unfeigned light. A part of the process is connecting one's self consciously to Source and to pursue our spiritual journey, at whatever point we are, and whatever faith we belong to. Over the years, Ataana developed a unique healing method, called The Ataana Healing Method, and established a Healing Center in Nashville, Tennessee, where he shares his gifts in personal sessions, workshops and on Energy Works Radio. More information can be found at www.ataanamethod.com.

This book is the first publication in which Ataana Badilli shares his spiritual wisdom and metaphysical experience, and one of his most powerful and cathartic tool for self-healing: *The Sacred Inner Dialogue*.

1. THE DEVELOPMENT OF THE SACRED INNER DIALOGUE

When I was nineteen years old, I did a Buddhist meditation. While chanting, I saw in front of me a very bright aquamarine topaz diamond-shaped gemstone right in front of my third eye, spinning in a high frequency. It made a sound by spinning really fast and that particular resonance had a vibration in it. It was a very high frequency sound. When it was right in front of my third eye, I had a feeling of being unified with my Source and I was feeling a warm and safe sensation in and around me.

That was the moment when I intuitively understood the deeper levels of karma, the karmic patterns and connections people have, and became temporarily integrated with my Enlightenment. This lasted for ten minutes, then the diamond-shaped aquamarine topaz gem moved far away to the horizon. That's when I understood the long journey that I still had to take to be in my Enlightenment.

After this experience, I was really sensitized towards karma, and activated in karmic knowledge. I understood karma and the laws of karma transformation. This is the reason that I know today why it's so efficient when we engage in Sacred Inner Dialogue. I know what your actions are causing in the bigger picture of karmic relations. I see the reprogramming of the blueprint, which SID makes possible, and I can inspire you on that path because I see the long-term effect.

Like an architect, I can support you to draw new energy pathways to create a new healthier blueprint for your life.

It took me years of experimenting to fine-tune the modality of Sacred Inner Dialogue to the exceptional healing tool that it is today. Now, I am using Sacred Inner Dialogue in my sessions with clients, and for myself, very effectively to shift patterns and balance blueprints with singular precision.

Here, I'd like to share with you how it all came about:

In my late twenties, I was in Germany studying natural medicine and on my way to being a naturopathic doctor. A colleague was fascinated with a modality centered around celebrating a person's feelings in small ceremonial sessions where time was dedicated to discuss emotions. I found it to be interesting. Over the years, I applied that approach often but found it not effective enough, because it was addressing an emotion without effectively creating or changing the inner structure of clients. Without changing their blueprint energetically, the same emotions would be re-lived over and over again.

I realized that an understanding of the ins and outs of human's inner communication processes was needed to produce effective long-term results. That was the moment when I began to create, by trial and error, SID. Success at the early stages meant to me already connecting a person to the idea of energy and inner processes, creating connections to his or her deeper states, which serves as a precursor to creating physical realities. I noticed that there was a whole energy system and infrastructure to subconscious intelligence in all of us that I could make visible. I developed that system over the next twenty years by experimenting and applying my findings. This evolved into ID and SID, an advanced self-empowered quantum healing system that supports us to navigate through our inner worlds and facilitate change in a more loving way.

Energy work and SID are the ideal combination to connect with infinite possibilities. It's like an x-ray system that utilizes all of our senses to see what is really happening inside of us. By asking specific questions, it can support us to access all of our inner and outer realities: past, present, future, and parallel.

SID can identify and make visible the blueprint of any person and it offers a map for anyone who truly wants to master this life's journey. It empowers us to redefine our reality by restructuring internal patterns. SID helps us to be more clear, connected, aware, responsible and accountable, and it allows us to understand the nature of our patterns. We can trace them back to their origins and recognize why we put these patterns in place. We're able to find the cause of the different forms of stagnation with SID and lovingly support the understanding of why they have been created, which then gives us enough fuel for forgiveness and healing to transform them completely.

SID shows us the depths of our existence and the deeper dialogues that are taking place within us. Please forgive my excitement in mentioning SID so often in this book. Also, forgive my "Germanisms" as German is my first language and this comes through in the way I verbalize my thoughts. I am so happy to work with this system that helps so many, that I emphasize it several times in this book, so you can really integrate it deeply. It's a self-awareness tool that gives us recognition—and with the right approach—it gives us also a good blueprint of who we really are, including all the way down to the level where the deeper and mostly unconscious processes that shape our thoughts and actions take place. SID helps us to accept our own truth and reality. For the participant and the practitioner, it is important to make the unhealthy patterns visible, so you can choose to lovingly release them from your belief systems and fill the newly formed spaces with healthy, life-affirming patterns.

I facilitate SID, workshops and group sessions. In addition, I teach SID. Working with me in a group allows all participants to process similar aspects that need self-healing and of which they were previously unaware. For instance, one person might bring up an unprocessed event from a previous relationship, and other participants might realize in that moment that they have remaining residue and work on it as well.

> *SID brings clarity to anyone wanting to know one's inner landscape or inner makeup. The inner makeup creates the outer reality, which in light of our outside experiences makes it easy to see what we need to change for a happier and healthier life. Since outside experiences are constantly mirrored back to us, we can with this understanding decide which patterns to change first, or in what order to approach a change of our patterns.*

As a practitioner, during SID, I provide clients with scripts to approach an aspect or a pattern that they desire to change. Sometimes I ask them to name it in their own words. These sentences contain the full spectrum structure of what we are addressing in our work. Sometimes I break it down into smaller pieces, if required. The scripts provide us with a bridge to the issues and give us direct access to them. If we can stay focused and complete the task, the scripts that we repeat, like affirmations, flow easy and create change.

We can apply SID to facilitate improvements or change in all of these areas: changes of profession, healing, letting go or improving relationships, raising income and prosperity levels, stress release, addiction-release, increasing Love and compassion levels, one's approach to life and improving our overall quality of life.

SID, in conjunction with the practitioner, can give you a really good grip on the multitude of different patterns that are simultaneously affecting different aspects within you. We can streamline and focus all patterns from different lives or life stages and can support a person to facilitate any change in this life through the use of SID.

With SID we realize that there is an inner dialogue happening at all times. SID is almost like a speech recognition software that recognizes something that was previously not visible, something that makes sound visible into words and vice versa, notes translated into sound or music, our sacred song. This is the inner dialogue that's happening in our system at all times which creates our reality. Once we take time to observe what's happening in our spiritual, mental, emotional and physical body, as well as energetically, like the thoughts and feelings that we dismissed many times in the past, we will realize the depth of our beings. SID will provide us very valuable access points for change.

When I first started energy work, I was more connected to radical transformation, applying raw energy to change a disharmony in my clients. These were miracle energy healings in which I worked intensely on a person on all levels in one session. However, this spontaneous healing cannot last if the person doesn't change. The disharmony can easily return unless a new infrastructure is in place. This is useful to remember:

> *We create disharmonies in our lives*
> *to make visible what is internally happening*
> *so we can learn from it and change it.*

Today I realize the real transformation lies in educating, remembering, and teaching what needs to be done or undone to live a better life.

As a practitioner, I can support you to navigate to the deepest points that are means to clearing your patterns faster. Working with a practitioner doesn't mean you can bypass a lesson altogether or evade the process, but it's rather comparable to the difference between going the distance like an average runner or like an Olympic runner who performs at a far higher level and has already won gold medals. You can be connected to the system to understand the process more efficiently and have your patterns lined up on a string so they are right in front of you. It's like the difference between diving for pearls in the ocean, collecting them one-by-one, and then stringing them to create a pearl necklace, or already having the pearl necklace presented to you in a gift box. Either way is fine, I love SID.

Since I am speaking here in this book to you as your own self-healer, and also to you as a potential practitioner of the SID modality with the goal to support others, I find it important to share one more profound benefit of using Sacred Inner Dialogue:

When I worked with clients without using SID, I would (just as you might do today) give energy healing sessions to my clients. During these sessions, I resolved things for my clients and they usually felt the immediate benefit from my work. I returned home and had energy residue from their sessions lingering with me for hours or even for days. I had effectively taken on their energies, and ended up working out their karma. I needed to combine sessions for my clients with extensive energy work on myself for the mere purpose to clear myself from these energies again!

Among the many people who are waking up at this time of our evolution, there are a great number of empaths who are dealing with a very similar problem on a daily basis: they pick up energies from other people and don't know what to do with these energies. SID allows empaths to clear themselves from energies that don't belong to them, and it allows practitioners not to pick up energies from others in the first place!

Once I introduced Sacred Inner Dialogue into the daily practice with my clients, SID allowed me to guide my clients to transform their energies themselves and to clear their own karma. Empowering my clients to work directly with their inner Self and to adjust their energetic blueprint to a healthier and more life-affirming state, allowed them to be actively involved in their healing process, and to experience their own power as creators of their own experiences. Besides these remarkable benefits for my clients, I was also able to support them in that process without taking on any unhealthy energies or karma.

Words have healing power.

Finally, before concluding this section on how Sacred Inner Dialogues came into existence, I want to call attention also to the most essential component of these dialogues: the words we speak.

In the Bible we read, "In the beginning was the Word, and the Word was with God, and the Word was God" (John 1:1). The word marks the moment of creation; in this verse the word is equated with the Creator Himself, i.e. with the one creative force in the universe. Words, and before words, intentions and energy have transformational creative power. They create something out of nothing, and transform what is already there. First, there is energy, then there is an idea, and then there is the spoken word that calls the material counterpart of the idea into existence.

It is a power that is known to many cultures and religions. There is a saying in India that equally illustrates the unique power of the word. It states that the Indian word Brahma, which is the name of the Hindu creator God and the first God of the trimurti, when pronounced in the right manner, will give you immediate access to Enlightenment, like the Buddhist mantras: Om Mani Padme Hum, Nam-myoho-renge-kyo. Also, like the 72 Names of God. These are examples of the power of the word and vibration, and I invite you to pay attention to all of your words because they also have creative power. Especially, the words spoken during Sacred Inner Dialogue can have immense impact on a person's life. The SID scripts in the chapters to come will show clearly their potential reach.

2. MEETING YOURSELF: ACKNOWLEDGING YOUR PROSPERITY BY GIVING VALUE TO YOURSELF

Imagine being in a safe place and I'm with you to navigate you to the depths of your being. I am helping you to see yourself for who you really are and what you're really doing, supporting you to realize that everything that is happening is inside of you, the chaos is within you, and that the vastitude, i.e. the unlimited possibilities of everything possible, is your very core. It is inside of you and also outside of you since it does not know any boundaries, and it can be accessed to facilitate healthy change. Any chaos you are experiencing can never be as deep as your core, sacred, light consciousness. Knowing this, there is no other intention than to allow your core light, your unlimited self, to express itself in the most sacred and healthy way. This insight will mark the turning point in resolving any problems or conflicts in your life.

Imagine yourself in a tiny submarine inside of yourself. There's an advanced sonar navigational system that's showing you your mental, emotional, spiritual, physical and energy states that you're in, what your heart or lungs look like, and what your spirit looks like. This navigational system is advanced enough to know through what lens you see yourself (positive, negative, neutral, current or from a past view point). These lenses can be cleared or adjusted.

It's advanced enough to create an overall route with pit stops for you to go in and come out in one session. You start to see an inner path and to realize what can be done to modify it and make the inside better. You see as much as you want to see, and you are ready to see more of who you are and who you can become. You are now connected to the All-Oneness, and can see your connections sparking eternally on the path of All- Oneness. What is important is intentionally connecting yourself to the infrastructure of All-Oneness because it illuminates a roadmap for you to activate your Energy irrigation and navigational systems for your journey back to wholeness.

As you dive deeper into yourself, you find fishnets on different parts of your chakra systems catching and trapping traumas and emotional residue. You see things on the inside that you're unable to see from the outside. What is not in order can now be identified and balanced. You see what roadblocks transpire, ready for you to see and clear them in advance.

It's as if you see yourself in a ship and there's a reef ahead of you and you know exactly where you're headed and how to handle the reef. We can identify the reef ahead of us as SID makes it become visible through energy and sound like an advanced sonar system.

Now we can see what's around us as if utilizing the most advanced radar and GPS system. Until you can fully see your inner world, a SID practitioner, and this book, can support you. It's like you're deep-sea diving, and if you feel you've gone to deep, you have a deep-sea diving instructor with you to bring you back to the surface, or to the right depth.

Understand, however, there is no limit to how deep you can go. You're unlimited, not bound by time or space. You're not limited to this life. You're not limited to ten past lives or a million lives. You are an unlimited being only limited by your believed limit, but sometimes you feel you can't handle your vastitude —that is the limitation. I can go through your connections to your Oneness and support you to seeing what needs to be seen and motivate you to transform the limitation.

This navigational system is not only addressing trauma and letting it go, it's also realizing the complexity of existence and who we are as human beings. Let's utilize this modality to support the understanding of life. It's about respecting everyone—including ourselves—wherever we are in the process, and seeing how far we can expand into our vastitude.

This way, we allow humanity to stop suppressing itself and start expressing itself in a healthy way. Once we stop suppressing ourselves, we stop suppressing others. Instead of feeding the anxiety an anxiety pill to suppress it, we're able to ask the anxiety, "What can I do for you?"

By acknowledging the trauma, we have just done something revolutionary. We've changed a pattern that humanity and our parents have taught us and imprinted in us. We transform ignorance into wanting to know. We transform suppressing into decompressing. That is a form of Enlightenment. We are moving from being afraid to looking deeper into having healthy communication with ourselves. We realize everything is infinite, including all emotions, situations and aspects of ourselves. It seems so simple that a child can do it. But once we understand the system we also understand the complexity of it. We can see and support ourselves better in unfolding and changing into who we really are or want to be.

When we think our thoughts are crazy and don't want to acknowledge them, we have to realize that this is suppression. Then we have to acknowledge the suppression and that the thoughts are a form of expression. When you think or say, "Well, I better not say this" or "I better not share that," and you start realizing this is a repetitive experience that's happening often, then you have to start acknowledging it. Once you acknowledge it, you can ardently change it. Acknowledging your already existing inner dialogue is the essence of every Sacred Inner Dialogue. Acknowledgment gives it value:

> *By acknowledging these inner processes,*
> *you're acknowledging prosperity*
> *because you give yourself value.*

3. EVERYTHING IS CONNECTED TO THE DIVINE

Everything is connected to the divine so are our inner thoughts. Acknowledgment activates your prosperity and you give yourself value, signaling to the universe that you're valuable. Therefore, the universe is going to send more valuable situations or things to you. At the same time, acknowledging our inner processes provide us with the opportunity to rewrite them, to restructure them. We're making previously invisible structures visible. It's not about me showing you the inner structures—but embolden you to discover them, I'm shining a spotlight, and you're starting now to see it for yourself and recognize deeper processes happening in you while before you, yourself dismissed them. And how did you learn to dismiss them? People important to you may have dismissed them: maybe your parents, friends, sisters, brothers, or whomever you grew up with ignored your feelings and their own feelings and you learned to do the same.

How many people in your life have been concerned enough with you to acknowledge and respect every one of your most inner processes and listen to all of them? Most likely what you have heard is, "This is stupid. This is silly. Shut up. Don't do this. This is not important. We don't have time for that. We have to do that instead of what you want." These messages created patterns, that many people still have in their heads running on repeat deep in their subconscious. These are some patterns which we grew up with.

Decades later, they often still suppress our creativity and freedom. Acknowledging them, accepting their existence, and attributing value to them, as constitutive parts of our life experience so far, allows us to break free from suppression and stuck-ness. Now we can create what we truly desire.

When we apply SID, we stop telling ourselves, "Shut up. It's not important." Instead, we want to know exactly what we are thinking because we see the value in our undivided life force and we recognize its ability to rewrite the patterns.

Think about it like this. It's the same as having the most amazing computer and running a software program on that computer that is no longer up-to-date. SID is supporting you with the newest software updates possible in the Multiverse in which we live.

A. HOW TO LEAD A SACRED INNER DIALOGUE (SID)

When we talk about the energy of desperation, for example, it's like a software program that is running on your computer. It makes you feel a certain way. If you cannot connect to the energy of desperation immediately, look deeper inside of you and you will find it. Now that being said, think about a situation in your life, which makes you feel hopeless, the one situation that you feel you can't change, that you feel desperate about. Now connect with it. With SID, we are basically addressing that software in your system by asking it if it can hear you. This is how we establish contact.

We say, "The energy of desperation in my life, can you hear me?"

Try it for yourself. Close your eyes. Take a deep inhale then slowly exhale.

Ask out loud, "My energy of desperation, can you hear me?"

Now observe if you get an energy sensation, hear a yes or no, see a color or feel sudden goosebumps.

If you get a response, great. If not, try it once more until you get a response, because everyone feels, in certain moments, desperate. Without ever clearing it, the energy of desperation is still somewhere in our system, and it will respond sooner or later.

After you get a response say, "My energy of desperation please start the transformational process and give me more space."

Your eyes are still closed and you're breathing deeply.

These words, spoken with sincerity—"My energy of desperation please start the transformational process and give me more space"— will wipe the hard drive and give you more space so you can put new software on your computer.

We're now replacing the software of desperation with a healthier software or belief system by saying, " The space that was occupied by the energy of desperation, can you hear me?"

Once you get an answer like yes, no or an energy response like goose bumps, it means it can hear you.

Then say, "I now fill the space that was occupied by the energy of desperation with the energy of ideal solutions and trust."

We just transformed the energy of desperation. Observe the energy shift. The space that just became available through the transformational process is now filled with the energy of ideal solutions and trust that will take care of any chronic problems. We effectively changed our programming from desperation to ideal solutions and trust. Repeat this process as often as needed. Can it be that easy? Love? Trust and flow!

We just transformed the energy of desperation. The space that became available through the transformational process is now filled with the energy of trust. We effectively changed our programming from desperation to trust.

We can now focus on the next unhealthy software program or belief system. For this demonstration, let's take on another equally universal experience, the experience of not feeling grounded and connected to Mother Earth.

Now close your eyes again and breathe deeply.

Say out loud, "My ungroundedness, can you hear me?"

Once we get a response, like in the previous example, we say, "My ungroundedness, please start the transformational process and give me more space."

"The space that just became available, can you hear me?"

Once we feel the transformational process starting and the space becoming available, we then ask the space, "Space, please be filled with healthy grounding and connectedness to Mother Earth."

To reemphasize our connectedness, we say, "Me being fully grounded and connected to Mother Earth, can you hear me?"

Once we get a response, we say, "Me being fully grounded and connected to Mother Earth, please become fully present in my everyday life."

It's like working with the energy system of a computer. The computer needs to be grounded in the earth. When we plug it in, we want to make sure there is no overcharge or overload of energy. Our physical energy system needs to be connected to Mother Earth in order to be healthy and well-balanced. The key here is that we see why the system is not already in that state, why it is not grounded and how to ground it. Clearing out the old, and inviting what we perceive as missing to become fully present in our lives is frequently all that is needed to effect a fundamental change.

B. REFLECTIONS

When I came to understand that energetic patterns are like software programs that contain life force and are programmed by us, it didn't make sense for me to work on anything else anymore. That's when I made transformational energy work the focus of my life.

Each person's blueprint is a network of learned software programs creating internal and external manifestations. I now focus on observing how energy is flowing, like a water irrigation system. Where does it need to be unclogged or redirected in order to reach even the most remote, delicate plants in our system? I look deep into all of that through my Multidimensionality lens and enjoy the possibilities and the vastness of it all.

SID is designed to harmonize and balance the chakra system by balancing ourselves with the earth, with stars, the Universe, God, Oneness, and our Source.

We are to look inward and question why self-worth, self-love and self-acceptance are not being allowed to have more space in our being. We inherit certain patterns and habits from our lineage or see as children from others what we then accept as reality. We say, "This must be important because so many people are doing this," and it becomes part of our belief system regardless of whether it's of a low frequency that will compromise us or of a high, life-supporting frequency that will bring out the best in us.

Have you seen the movie the matrix when Neo was offered the red or blue pill by Morpheus? He chooses the red one, so he can stay in wonderland to see deeper into the Matrix reality! Or the movie, Dances with Wolves? Kevin Costner was chasing the wolf and the Native American Indians were laughing and saying, "He's crazy!" until the Shaman says to them, "He is dancing with the wolf."

He was chasing the wolf away but when the Shaman was looking at the situation, he saw a being that was actually dancing with the wolf.

A situation may look crazy from the outside but when we look at it from an aligned deeper understanding, it looks different. Such deeper understanding is required for us on a daily basis. SID is giving us this sacred inner view. The sacred inner dialogue gets us to the sacred inner view because we're seeing so much more with the sacred eyes of the initiate or Shaman.

It might look like, "Hey this is crazy!" He's doing something that doesn't make any sense because we haven't attributed any sense to a particular behavior. We are not looking at it right unless we look at it with wonder, true interest, and through the eyes of loving Oneness. Looking at it from the mundane, boring lens of expectation is looking at it without sacredness. When the Shaman looks at it, he is in awe of the situation and with curiosity says, "What is this guy really doing?" What is the sacred truth here?

And then the Shaman says, "He's dancing with the wolf, don't you see it?"

It's like the Bible has it, *Be like children.* We are to look at life with wonder, through the eyes of children. We ought to be looking at our life with curiosity, observation and experimentation.

Sacred inner dialogue helps you identify what you're truly seeing and with what energy a person is interacting with the Multiverse. That's how you truly see the inner interaction that the person has with the Multiverse. You see the real energy of that person's blueprint.

There is a Native American Indian saying that describes us all as unlimited star systems. It says the only thing we don't know or haven't experienced is limitation. That is why we are here on this planet, to integrate limitations, and to remember our vastness, because it's not a reality for us. In our hearts we know limitation is just partially true. Our striving for unlimitedness is best expressed here in one example of the Men's 100 Metres Sprint world record progressions. In 1906, the world record was 10.6 sec. In 2009, it was 9.58 sec. That gives you an idea how much closer we got to our unlimitedness. It took 100 years for humans in the 100 Metres Sprint to take about 1 sec off. I encourage you to look at the world record progressions of the different Olympic disciplines. Where is that going to end and what is the goal here? If the trend prevails, we are going to be, in 900 years or earlier, already at the finish line by just merely having the intention to be there. That's immediate manifestation. In other words, unlimited speed or infinite speed. Marathon world record progressions are even more dramatic from 1926, 3:40:22 to 2:02:57 in 2014. That is a whopping 1hour 37min. faster than 88 years ago.

When I refer to Multidimensionality, it's a reference that parts of our selves are present everywhere in this universe in all dimensions. The Oneness, for example, think of it as a pie, where we are present in all slices of that pie as ingredients. We are present in one form or another in all of the slices. When I accentuate Oneness, or Multidimensionality, it is because the whole Energy system of All of Existence (now think Big) can be accessed because we are part of it. Multidimensionality is to be fully consciously present in this moment, fully expanded into all realities, and fully aware. There is a theory that all actions are simultaneously unfolding into infinity on all levels and create every possible outcome, each outcome is a different reality dimension. The question is, what dimensions are we resonating with the most? We can adjust our experience to the desired journey and outcome by energetically aligning ourselves with it.

When you look at us, we are all unlimited energy beings, and we are all creators of our reality, or co-creators at least. There is a reason why we are experiencing what we are experiencing. That means we are in power and in charge of understanding our relationship to any energetic pattern. By us merely saying, "Go away. Just transform. Just leave me alone. Just be gone," we express with these power phrases that we want to push it away and do not really wish to deal with it. This is not a solution because we manifested the situation for a reason. If we just want to push it away, or be impatient with it, this means we haven't accepted our role in the co-creation. It means we're not fully taking responsibility for our actions, so, most likely, we haven't learned what we need to learn. Chances are, it's not going to be released or go away.

C. A GENTLER SID-SCRIPT

Sometimes I apply a gentler script for a Sacred Inner Dialogue. For example, when asking pain to start the transformational process, I sometimes ask the pain to give you more space.

Some problems can be addressed immediately while others still need to ripen. Sometimes you can't fully karmically approach a condition until you feel and truly accept it, ultimately, all the way back to its origin. We strive to totally understand our condition, which means frequently knowing in depth about a past life. Sometimes we need more space before we can go there. We can't approach a condition fully because it's not fully approachable yet. There's still too much going on for it to completely be released.

For example, if someone has cancer and you immediately ask the cancer to start the transformational process, without an introduction, without seeing its background and the origin of its toxicity (whether it's physical, mental, spiritual or emotional), then it doesn't give you full access when approaching it. In this case, you don't even have the level of compassion needed to access the issue if you simply ask it to, "Just transform".

You can't just go with the most powerful words—they're not going to help if you're not going to look for and acknowledge the reason or cause as to why you created a condition in the first place. A condition is truly being resolved karmically when you say, "I'm approaching it with the utmost respect and love for myself and for what I created."

Then you have all the patience in the world to deal with it and that's when the condition will respond to you. If you're not patient with it, then you haven't received your full learning experience. We're unlimited timeless beings and have all the time in the world for everything we want to do. I learned my major lessons from the crystal gemstone beings when I approached them with openness, love and by having more than enough time dedicated to understand them. That was when these beings opened up to me, for example One Human lifetime in a crystal's growth process is equivalent to a sneeze for them. They grow in millions of years; if we approach them with a timetable, pressure, or stress, they are not going to answer us. The same goes for our karmic patterns and any of our past life's, they are ancient and deeply engrained in the depth of our beings. A crystal or a past life has been around for some time and without patience we are not reaching the proper momentum, compassion or zero point to access them.

When we get to a karmic understanding of a condition, we say, "Wow, that comes from such a deep place. It doesn't come from this life time. It comes from another lifetime." In this way, you're approaching it with much more care, respect and a wider and deeper understanding." —As if you wanted to bring something up to the surface from beneath the water. The deeper it is in the water, the deeper the breath has to be that we have to take to reach it in its depth. By doing that, you're giving it the space to transform—and you have, first of all, enough love and compassion for it. In exchange, this attitude allows the pattern to be fully considered and respected, and then it willingly will work with us.

With the karmic realization experience that I had with the Buddhist mantra, and the enlightening moment, I felt all of a sudden warmth, wholeness, care, coming home, and remembrance of my gifts. Similar to the time when I saw the Emerald Green Donut (EGD), which is a form of experiencing God's presence through geometrical shapes and colors. With this knowledge, I was able to see energy infrastructures. All of a sudden, I could see everything (the energy patterns, the karmic relationships people had and the flow of their energy). That's when I realized the connection between our energy blueprint and the physical manifestations in our lives.

When I work with Sacred Inner Dialogue, I'm looking deep into what's going on in a person's past life, parallel life, and current life with respect to their overall association to the Multiverse.

The presence of a practitioner is beneficial, especially at the beginning, when we wish to access deep patterns that might have originated lifetimes ago. However, everyone can do this. Everyone can look into the depth of themselves, into their own or someone else's life.

SID allows us to approach non-serving patterns from a holistic point of view. We can consider everything as accessible (what is happening now, current situations, opportunities, possibilities, past lives, future lives, business projects, relationships, personal life, and everything that we want to change).

We can heal our lives, and we can experience our lives as more joyful and prosperous. Yet, healing is different from "perfecting" our lives or ourselves. We are already ideal. We are already complete. We just have to remember that we are ideal and complete.

SID supports us to recognize what structure is in place and supports us to create a new healthy infrastructure and blueprint. It also supports us with the deeper aspects of shame, guilt and emotions that can be addressed immediately. This includes abandonment from Source, feeling rejected, not being connected, being separated from one's power, one's Source, from one's God or Goddess connection.

D. FINDING APPROVAL

We're going into a place where we can address our whole sacred system. If we look at all the religions, they all say we are made in the image of the Creator. I go even so far as to say we are the mirror image of the solar system. Our physical structure, the way our organs are laid out within our body, is similar to the layout of the planets and of suns and stars. We are literally made in the image of the galaxy and the Multiverse.

For example, if you feel hopeless or powerless you can simply activate your sun system in your solar plexus chakra and the sun power can truly work and manifest itself in you and bring back hope into your life. That's the power of consciousness that we possess.

When Krishna and Shiva were incarnated, they could touch an area on their body, go to the corresponding counterpart in the galaxy and be present there, almost like by virtue of a beaming device. Parts of us resonate and respond to parts of the Multiverse, and we can be anywhere we want to be. So lets be fully present here in this moment first to strengthen our life force.

Once we come to this planet and we incarnate in the body, we are pre-approved for unlimited amounts of abundance, opportunities, possibilities and happiness. The toughest part was coming here and becoming incarnated. Once incarnated, we are fully pre-approved for all things possible. We don't have to do much in terms of gaining further approval except to love and approve of ourselves. Once we realize this, we have access to unlimited resources.

I'm not saying this from a lazy person's point of view. Of course, we have to be willing to do everything needed for our purpose, but we come from the knowledge that everything is already available to us.

> *Ultimately it's about us approving of ourselves.*
> *We put the stamp of approval on ourselves.*

Let me be the quality control and approve of you now in this moment. Ultimately, you have already approved yourself. If you weren't pre-approved, you couldn't come through the wormhole and be born into this world. Nobody is sneaking in here. You are entering a big process and you are focused on being incarnated. The stars have to be right. Everything has to be aligned. You are born within a specific star alignment. It has information about your meaningful life, makeup and gifts you bring with you. Can you imagine the complex planning that is required for all beings to be born where they need to be? Very much like His Holiness the Dalai Lama, to know what family to be born into and to be found and recognized?

It is as if all the stars are giving you specific energies (Star light). It's interesting to see what part of the world people are choosing when they incarnate. The dial has to be put into the right place at the right time and then you can come in. There is no coincidence. Everything has to be lined up. Then, boom here you are. You're born. You've already done the fine mechanical work. The rest is actually living your life, being taken care of, and allowing your gifts to be shared.

Our existence on this planet is not about wondering, "What do I need to do to be approved by others?" That type of thinking makes us very vulnerable. When we look for outside approval, we can be very easily corrupted. When we approve of ourselves because we know who we are, we will receive approval without having to do anything that we don't want to do.

Let's look more deeply at our frequent attempts to gain approval, which are not needed. It's like when you're sitting in a restaurant and you're placing an order with the person sitting next to you. They respond, "Sure I can approve and take your order, but your order isn't going to go through because you haven't put your order in with the waiter. I'm not the waiter, but I sure appreciate you giving me the opportunity to approve or disapprove of your choice."

People can say, "Yeah, we're approving of you", but the only approval you ultimately need is your own approval. Ultimately, you are the whole scenario: the waiter, the owner, the chef and the person next to you. The channel of approval is one's self and the only approval needed is self-approval.

In fact, you need to recognize that you're already pre-approved. You're going around and looking for approval from everywhere outside of you and that approval is not doing anything for you because it's empty and only temporarily satisfying. You still don't feel approved even if a hundred million people approve of you. The only thing that's happening is that you are filling the empty space inside you for a fleeting moment until the need for approval arises again. And it will arise again and again until we approve of ourselves.

It's the same with actors and actresses who go to auditions to be cast for a role. The director and producer sit there and say, "This person is not a good fit for this role. We're going to cast another person for this role to see if that person is a better fit."

This sets up actors and actresses to learn about rejection. They are being rejected and rejected and rejected and ultimately becoming adept of rejection and approval. By the time an actor receives one role, he has auditioned for a hundred roles, or was lucky with connections to get the first role. Anytime there's an audition, there's the huge risk of being rejected because another hundred people want the same role.

You're stressed all the time because you have to prove yourself in front of a hundred other people who also want that job. What makes you better than these people?

They are likely just as good as you are which means you are facing constantly the risk of very serious and possibly even higher levels of probable rejection.

Actors and actresses experience this and become masters of rejection. The moment they say, "I don't care if I'm rejected or not," and they're not taking it as serious or personal anymore, that's when they're becoming successful. And guess what? They're receiving approval later on in their careers by others because, at the same time, they become masters of approval.

When you make a good movie and it's successful, all of a sudden everyone is approving of you and everyone wants to be around you.

It's the same with standing in front of the people who say yes or no to your audition. You're doing your best but you're not depending on that approval. Once you start approving of yourself, all good things will come to you.

That means you have to approve of yourself first. When you're not afraid of rejection anymore, and you are going after a part, you're not trying to avoid the negative charge anymore. You can enjoy the experience. The situation doesn't have an emotional disappointment value associated with it because it doesn't do anything for or against you. It's like you driving your car and are already late to a very important meeting, but have to stop at a red light. This doesn't happen to you because you're a bad person, or the light chose to sabotage or reject you. No, these are the steps of participating in traffic. Let me ask you, isn't traffic sometimes an amazing teacher to mirror to us where we are in life?

The more you audition, the better you get. The less you're afraid, the better you deal with rejection, the less it's going to hurt you and the more relaxed you're going to be.

Once you get better in learning your craft, you go in there, you show up, and it may fit you or it may not. You might meet another person who makes your day better, or the audition is a good experience in life. It can be a good day even if you don't receive the role.

You remain in your power, rather than participating in any conflict by saying, "If I don't get this, it's because I'm not good enough, or I'm not looking this way or that way." There's no need to start the inner "loser dialogue". Instead, enjoy being out there and enjoy having the opportunity to learn, to experience, and to be joyful, all while getting better at the craft and instead of the "loser dialogue" start the Sacred Inner Dialogue.

Your art does not depend on anything else when you're already pre-approved. The good things are starting to find you because you removed the obstacles, the angst is gone. The moment you still feel the need for approval, you're giving your power away. The more you get out there in front of the world (it doesn't matter what they think about you!), the more you're approving of yourself. That's important. You know who you are. You are subconsciously giving the people around you instructions on how to approach and treat you. Start remembering your full potential, approve and improve on a daily basis.

When you know who you are, another person's judgment doesn't negatively affect you because no other person can define you. Your actions, your thoughts, your service, your love, your beingness is defining you, not someone else. We carry this sense of unconditional and unlimited approval in ourselves. When we recognize this and activate it, we're going to be approved by ourselves and by the Multiverse.

When you realize that you are already pre-approved and you are simply focused on approving yourself, you're letting go of a whole lot of stress.

It is about energy. The energy of approval is a high frequency. When somebody approves of you, lets say a bank or an Investor, access to Funds and resources for your projects are effortless. You now are in possession of a beautiful certainty: You know that you don't have to waste your energy with proving yourself constantly to the investor or bank. You're already approved for that loan. This frequency of approval is a big deal because it gives you access to experiencing a whole lot of expansion, space and leverage. Sooner or later, you will rejoice in yourself and fill this space with your own approval.

However, the more people impute approval on you, the more you can gain space to approve of yourself, too. Either way, you are going to get there, but it's a whole lot more work if you constantly believe that you have to do something for someone else first. That's particularly troublesome because there is nothing perfect you can do long-term for anybody because nobody can make it better for themselves other than that very person herself or himself, and that makes gaining long-term approval from others a most unrealistic goal.

We can do something in a perfect way for somebody, but a person can still do it better on their own. Until one has done it for oneself, one cannot fully show his own self-love to one's self. It doesn't matter if you love someone dearly and do everything for them, it's never going to be as valuable as it is when they are really with kindness lovingly doing it for themselves.

You're going to get close but it's not going to be perfect, and thus, you're not going to be ever feeling satisfied or be fully approved. That person is going to judge and say, "It was good, but not perfect."

When people depend on other people's approval, it's never really going to pan out because ultimately that approval is always going to be sour. You hear responses such as, "It was good, but this and that could have been done better. I would have done it this way or that way. It's not satisfying."

That's why Sacred Inner Dialogue is one of the most powerful tools today in the healing world. It gives us an easy access to whatever is happening in the moment. We can identify it and actually address it. As we're addressing it, we can start modifying and streamlining our life to the ideal life we want to experience.

The key to understanding the protocol with SID is to first understand how it works when the system works on ourselves, from the inside. Then we observe our responses to the questions, "What emotions are we feeling? What energies are we feeling? What physical, emotional, mental, spiritual, astral sensations do we have at the moment, right now?" Then we start to acknowledge our thoughts, feelings and emotions. We first have to acknowledge them before SID gives us access. It's like a car that rolls down the street, for which we don't have the key. The solution is finding the key to get into it, stop it, and drive it in the desired direction by taking responsibility for our lives.

By taking responsibility, we acknowledge that we have access to our own car. If we just hold the key in our hands and the car rolls down the road, nothing happens. The moment we take responsibility, acknowledge it, and step forward, we utilize the key and say, "Hey, I acknowledge I have the key to my car." Then we jump into the car. We slam on the brakes. And guess what? We stop the car and begin driving it in the right direction—wherever we want it to go.

The moment we take responsibility, acknowledge it and step forward, we utilize the key and say, "This is my car." Once we claim it, change happens. That's when we can drive it in a different direction. We first have to take responsibility and acknowledge the pattern, and then we can start directing our lives in a better direction. Rather than thinking, "This is an awful pattern—let's just transform it and let it go," it is important that we acknowledge the situation from a place of Oneness and compassion.

Look at it. Acknowledge it. Lovingly and respectfully transform it.

Why? Because love is the key in the first place.

E. RECLAIMING YOUR SPACE (PARASITES)

Love (for yourself), loving, respectful transformation, and determination are the keys to deal with parasites. Keep in mind, parasitism is a classic type of relationship in the organic world. It denotes a one-sided energetic transaction that leads to the exhaustion of the host and happens for the benefit of the parasite. Energetic parasitism, or parasitism, describes such relationships. When people have parasites and just want to kill the parasites, they're bringing death energy into themselves. It's better to claim back the space that the parasites occupied and acknowledge that the parasites are there for a reason: because you invited them. You may say, "Well I'm probably not going to be an athlete, writer, actor, artist, musician, energy healer or painter," so the parasites respond, "Since she's not going to be a famous painter or musician or Energy Healer, that space (that part of her life force) is available," and they ask the Universe if they can be in that place.

This is a user friendly Universe.

The Universe says, "Sure, as long as she's not using that space, you can be there." Then the parasites occupy the space and after five years you say, "I'm changing my plans. I want to be a musician," but you are lacking access to your own energetic resources for realizing your dream because the parasites bog down your system.

The parasites reply, "That wasn't the plan. You didn't want to be an artist at all." Now you have to convince the parasites that you do want to be a musician. That means you want to put energy and resources into becoming an artist. By saying it, you are claiming that space to be an artist or activating your artistic abilities, which means you're planning to reclaim that space. Once you convince the parasites you really want to be there, you will get there.

Remember, the parasites are already established there, in your energy field; it is their home, too. Let's say they've been occupying your space for five years. The parasites think it's their home for eternity. Once you proclaim with really strong intention, "I truly want to be that actor, actress or musician or whatever it is that you want to be and feel passionately about," then you have to stand your ground more than the parasites that have been established for five years. Say, "You know what? I'm going to stick it out. I really want to do it." Then you really have to start claiming that space by acting on your intention.

There's no empty space in the Universe. The Universe says yes to everything, including parasites.

"Yeah, you can go there," the Universe says to the parasites, "as long as you're giving back that space when it's required, you can have it."

But what is the extent of space recall that is required? In order to succeed, it needs to be a complete recall of all of my space. What do you have to do to convince the parasites that you really want to have all of that space now?

The parasites think, "No, you're not serious. You just want to do this for one or two weeks and then you're going to stop. We won't let you push us out for two weeks of passion. We'll be out of here and that's not good. Show me that you really want it!"

So how do you show it? With perseverance. Working on parasites clearing, for example, is really moving your energies on doing what your passion is. The first thing you do with the Sacred Inner Dialogue is start a dialogue with the parasites. Initially, the parasites are not going to believe you and then you're going to say with more conviction, "I'm very certain that I want to do it." The parasites still say, "Show us."

The next day you take piano lessons. The following day you take singing lessons. The parasites say, " That's iffy, let's see if you can do this for two months." Then your perseverance comes through and you succeed. You become a success, and successful at perseverance and at following your passion. That's when the parasites say, "We trust you. We believe you. We will give you that space back." And you will be moved to tears, realizing how they actually supported you by challenging you to step into your power.

There's a way and form of how you can successfully communicate, "I'm taking my power back." This is an example of understanding why a scenario like that happens. In the beginning, we feel we're not going to use the full potential of our being. That's why there is candida, yeast, fungus or parasites in our system. They occupy space we wouldn't normally use. Most of the time when we have parasites, attachments of energetic entities, and feel alone, we feel stronger by having that kind of support. (After all, they fill emptiness inside us.) When we invite entities, we are typically not cognizant of that fact that we are extending an invitation to them. We simply don't use our full potential, which is sufficient for others to feel invited to use that part of our life force that we neglect. Or we wish to overcome emptiness inside us, and accept parasitical relationships to meet this need.

Sometimes we did it when we were nine or ten years old; we attracted these entities into our lives or they were passed on to us from the family lineage. These entities are often with us because we didn't want to feel alone, which is not a bad thing. We called them in because we didn't want to be alone, but now we just want to get rid of them. I'm not saying all the entities are similar, some entities want space, some entities want life force. Sometimes having entities reflects a belief system of personal inadequacy and this belief system invites entities to occupy our space. Then we have to claim our space back from entities like parasites.

Parasites are a little smarter than we think and have the ability to start communicating, too. We start a dialogue with the entities to free up space so we can truly move forward with our lives. That means also SID helps to recognize and empower our unlimited self and the power of creation or co-creation of ourselves. We are not merely victims, but responsible and powerful co-creators of our reality.

4. PROTOCOL FOR SACRED INNER DIALOGUES: MODEL-SID FOR ADDRESSING FEAR AND PROCRASTINATION

In the following, I will be talking about what *I* am doing, and what *you* need to do during SID, and what *we* do and say. This structure is reflective of the fact that you can engage in a SID by yourself or assisted by a practitioner like myself, and depending on the situation, it will be you who asks the questions, or I might assist you in doing that.

The protocol for SID asks you first to be relaxed. You can sit or lay down. Close your eyes for a moment, breathe deeply and give yourself permission to bring your attention to the center of your head. Then you're asked to be open to any answers that come to you after asking a question. For example, if you're asking the energy of procrastination if it can hear you, I'm also asking you to be very observant if there's an energy response, such as a physical response, a mental response, or an emotional response with a yes or no; perhaps there are also goosebumps or even a color that might emerge in front of your eyes. You are asked to identify any type of response you are receiving.

Once you are getting a response in form of a sensation, you need to acknowledge that response. Ask the same question one more time to see whether that response persists. Then ask a third time and be very certain that the issue is responding. Once it responds clearly, we can start investigating. We can ask with love and respect, "Is there anything I can do for you?"

If someone asks fear, "Fear, can you hear me?" and the energy of fear answers, and the person feels a panic attack, then ask the fear to give you more space so that we can remedy the momentary situation, allowing us to start the uncovering of the deeper issues and identifying the source of the energy response.

We can ask fear if there's anything it would like to share with us or if there's anything we can do for it. "Fear, is there anything I can do for you?" Fear is there for a reason. What is the reason?

Fear might respond back and say, "You need me for your protection." Then you would say, "Why do I need you for protection?"

Fear: Because you're going to be confronted with this or that.

The key is to remain attentive and focused on whatever the root cause of our fear is. Therefore we continue our investigation and ask, "What is it that I need to be protected from?" Let's say, my success, if I'm afraid of success because it can change my life, then I don't want it seriously because of the unknown situation that success will bring into my life. I might be afraid of attributing great importance to myself, and thereby changing the status quo. In that case, my fear is protecting me from success and from the change that would come with success.

Fear is not really the issue.

"For years I have been suffering from fear for no reason. The real cause is success and change."

As I'm going deeper, I'm asking fear, "Is there anything that I can do for you?" And you are asking fear again, "Fear is there anything that I can do for you?" Then fear says, "Deal with success. Accept change." Once it says to me, "accept change," I am ready for the next step.

I will now confront my fear with my willingness to accept success and change (or accept whatever the cause for my fear might have been), which will allow for the dissolution of the fear. Once I feel ready to fully accept and welcome into my life what I was afraid of before (as evidenced by the presence of my fear), I speak:

"My acceptance of change and success, can you hear me?" When it says "yes", I continue: "Acceptance of change and success, come with me to the fear."

Why?

Because that's the code for fear to dissolve. When I stand in the energy of full acceptance with the formerly deemed "fear-inducing" issue in front of my fear, then the fear starts transforming by itself. Without having pushed the fear, without having created resistance, or doing anything other than desiring to learn about the deeper aspects of why it's there, I am able to lovingly dissolve this fear by demonstrating that it is no longer needed.

It is important to note that, in order for the code to be effective, it has to be recognizing the root cause of why the issue is there. It has to connect and resonate.

At this point, I recommend you to implement an affirmation:

"I now lovingly accept success and change in my life."

Repeat this affirmation for the next sixty-five days to take care of any remnants of the fear.

5. PAST LIVES

It's a fairly normal—and to be expected—process for past lives to come up during a SID session. They come up so that they can be recognized as well. That's often the case when we work with crystals or Sacred Inner Dialogue. The reason why they come up is because you now have the tools to work on them; that's why your subconscious pushes them up to the surface. As long as you don't have the tools, your subconscious doesn't give you access to work on them. It might be now that you're open to seeing past life issues because you're contemplating energy systems. Because you are developing an understanding of the inter-connectedness of your present, past future, and parallel lives including of all there is (Oneness).

Your system says, "Its time now to deal
with it, you have the right tools, lovingly
change dysfunctional programs."

A. PAST PERSECUTION FOR BEING A HEALER

Almost all healers have experienced in one or more of their past lives accusation of wrongdoing and being persecuted because of their gifts. For instance, they might have been burned on the stake as witches under the Inquisition. Many have suffered discrimination, persecution, and loss of their lives for practicing healing, or they died for their beliefs. During the Inquisition, the Catholic Church didn't tolerate what was perceived as competition to or subversion of their authority and principles, which resulted in hundreds of thousands of people being burned at the stake. There are many healers alive now who had past lives where they were either burned as a healer or involved in burning healers.

That is a past life experience that is very traumatic. People were victimized by not being able to speak up for their beliefs and convictions. Many healers felt, and might still feel today, that they could not openly pursue their healing work due to such a harrowing past in which they still carry a subconscious memory. The trauma is stemming from being lynched for what they believed in, which was healing. They were helping and healing themselves and others, but instead of receiving recognition for their service, they were persecuted or even burned at the stake.

Speaking to you, to a community of present-day healers, it is safe for me to say that each one of us goes through past life experiences and stages that involve the memory of torture and persecution. Most people who work with Sacred Inner Dialogues and are exploring deeper levels of this healing technique tap into experiences where they suffered tremendously because of their beliefs.

The same happened to early Christians. They found themselves in a situation, in which they decided, "We will become martyrs for what we believe in,"—similar to Jesus Christ who showed up to lead people through different stages of ascension. The stages were: You go. You experience. You heal. You will be hated. You will be disowned. You will be tortured, crucified, killed—and then you're going to be free. It's almost like a "coming out of the closet" - manual. After a while, you say who you are and people start hating you, and then you'll get to this place where you're all of a sudden free of everything and you don't put any importance on other people's approval.

I'd also wish to bring to mind that our subconscious memory of the past life trauma can have a broad range of implications on our current life. It is helpful for us to understand them, and to bring healing to these parts of our personality. For instance, in a past life when accused of being a witch, a person was burned. Today, this person could be afraid of fire. In another past life, trauma was experienced by drowning, which could be why a person is afraid of water in this lifetime.

These are all memorized patterns and limitations in the system that we can address.

If you know someone was executed by the Inquisition in their past life, you can imagine they have problems with their throat chakra. Because they wanted to speak out for healing, but weren't allowed to express themselves, and when they did they were executed. Projections were made onto them, casting them as being malicious and other than healers. This person wants to help people but in another lifetime he or she was told you are a bad evil person. This can, in a current life, present a conflict because they feel resentment about utilizing their healing abilities and don't know if they want to be a health practitioner at all. They struggle between not knowing if they should do this or not do this because in a past life they were agonized. The Clash song comes to mind, "should I stay or should I go?" Even if they're suffering because their inner calling for healing comes to the forefront of their lives, they don't want to take on the responsibility anymore because they're traumatized from the past.

This can show up during a SID session or even for some who read this book. However, SID can easily be utilized in these to transform such past trauma, also healing crystals can be added to speed up the self-healing process.

Here are some examples of affirmations to claim your Energy healing power:

> I'm now ready to claim all of my power.
>
> I'm ready to take all of my power back.
>
> I'm now fully present in my purpose.
>
> I am safe at all times, I now claim my power and express all of my gifts.

B. TRAUMA FROM OTHER PAST LIVES AND UNDERSTANDING ARCHETYPAL PATTERNS

The same mechanism of conditioning through past life traumas that we could see with having been persecuted as a healer in the past, applies equally to past lives of being the king, being the queen, being the empress, the emperor. It applies to having lived in a suppressed state, such as a slave or concubine setting. It applies to the warrior setting, to being the victor as well as to being steamrolled by another country. All of these experiences are past life experiences that will shape our current life experience. To give an illustration: It had been so traumatizing because you can imagine being the king or queen of a country and your advisors say, "You really need to go to war with another country," but you are not up to par, and the other country wins. You end up losing hundreds or thousands or millions of your subjects or soldiers and you might then be exiled or executed because of that advice. That's a trauma that people have who don't want power in this lifetime; for example, they shy away from power because they had been involved in the destruction of civilizations like Atlantis.

I also want to bring your attention to a trauma that some men have in this lifetime by having been kept captive by Amazons in a past life; they were kept in cages and abused for reproductive purposes, what in exchange made them fearful of powerful women and they consequently strove to suppress these women in this lifetime.

The abuse that is still memorized from a past life is a big deal. It has to be dealt with sooner or later. It can be as recent as "World War II" and be as far back as Egypt, Greece, Rome, Sumer, Atlantis, Lemuria or civilizations that came long before us, as well as experiences in extraterrestrial worlds.

It's like being in one media room with a thousand screens, where one or several of these past, parallel, future, multidimensional lives are being played at the same time. With SID, we have access to watch and intercept any one of these movies and create a different outcome. You know how you can change outcomes with movie DVDs lately? You can basically stop and select a different ending. You can say, "This is a little violent, I want to change the ending." You can change any of the past lives in a similar manner, and each change will effect a different experience overall. Everything is like cogs feeding into each other, creating movement. What then moves in this lifetime creates a different reality.

That's what I do when I practice my modality and assist my clients. When we work on a life, I see the overall effects of every little action. I see the rippling effect of each action unfolding while creating a new narrative picture. Like a spectator, you can now pull back from all the screens and you see the screens all together creating an entirely different image, almost like a media puzzle. When you look at it, you have a thousand small images of something and all of a sudden you look from a distance and it looks like a cathedral, or it looks like a very clear outline of a person's face.

But when you look closer, it looks like pieces and pixels of something else. I can see from the inside to the outside from the distance and the closeness. I can see the transformation that occurs in the overall evolution, and how new harmony expresses itself. With Sacred Inner Dialogue, I can support the overall transformation. That's why it's so important and beneficial for people to learn SID to the fullest, so that ultimately, the key to not only changing a tiny corner of a pixel from the left or the right, but the overall picture will be in their hands.

In that way, when we allow these past lives to come up—and they can come up automatically when we're working with Sacred Inner Dialogue—we can translate them from there all the way back to us and support their transformation.

When we look into these archetypes and they reveal themselves to us we can support the self-healing process.

There are twelve common archetypes. Taking this seriously, we recognize: Anyone in a civilization can mirror back to us a past life that we once lived or experienced ourselves. The development of civilizations as well as our individual ascension process over multiple lifetimes depends on experiencing all sorts of archetypes who become for us like building blocks for our soul's growth process and education.

Ultimately, anything that is part of the experience of humanity is a form of Archetypal past life experience. We all benefit from being open to explore our own relationships to other people and to the archetypes they represent.

C. SID AND UNDERSTANDING HUMAN EXPERIENCES

There are people from all types of different places who have faced all kinds of struggles that have happened in many different lifetimes.

This is not to place blame and make us feel good or bad, it's knowing there's a memory that goes with an experience and that it is the memory of a traumatic experience that has to start the healing process. When we ask these past lives in Sacred Inner Dialogues and they respond to us, we want to make sure we are approaching and addressing them in a way that supports the healing process. I want us to start looking at the full spectrum of experiences and their consequences for our personal development over multiple lifetimes in order to understand what we are going through in this lifetime. The energies, events, experiences that upset us in our everyday life, most likely stem from a past life. We can address trauma through a simple process that starts with the following statement:

"My past life, can you hear me?"

Then, when it answers with "Yes" or an energy response, we can say:

"My past life, start the self-healing process."

"My past life, please reveal more about yourself."

Then we can go deeper into that past life and approach it in a way that allows us to really figure out what was going on at that time. Once we have more insight, we can start approaching it with understanding, love and compassion, which gives us a sense of power rather than perceiving ourselves as victims of that past life. And in that moment, we have already begun to transform the traumatic experience.

When you find out, for example, that you lived a past life during the Inquisition and experienced torture and hurt in so many different ways, and still feel the pain of being tortured today, the experience needs to start the healing process on many different levels.

This means for us not being afraid to look at the whole picture because that's when you can gain full overview and deepest insight. It might hurt for a moment but you will ultimately have full insight into all aspects of the traumatic experience that you are transforming through SID.

You can actually go into your whole past life and ask the past life to start the self-healing process. There's so much trauma in that past life and it's not just one single traumatic experience. You've been tortured, forced to say something you didn't want to say, or forced to do something you didn't want to do, you were made to feel guilty, you were suppressed, or you basically bought yourself free by betraying your beliefs.

Even if that was not a first-hand experience, but let's say a child saw this happening to their mother who was burned at the stake. Do you think this child wants to go into experiencing more of their own gifts? Not in a million years! But with SID, it is easy to unlock these gifts and activate the willingness to want to do so.

If you're being related in any way to a sacred healing circle and that happened to someone in the healing circle, you can imagine the other members saying, "No, we don't want to be part of that healing circle anymore."

The same could be witnessed at Christ's crucifixion. Can you imagine, you walk with Christ and have this amazing being and his amazing energy right next to you, and the crucifixion brings the sudden loss of your connection with this being in the physical form. You must have felt an incredible sense of abandonment and loss. This trauma of having been near spiritual Enlightenment and having it taken away must be intense. That could be the reason for seeking out spiritual Enlightenment in another lifetime, or for staying away from it as not to repeat that loss.

Once you understand the dynamics of past lives, we can use Sacred Inner Dialogue and ask, "Any torture that I experienced from my past life, under the Inquisition, can you hear me?" Once we address it and it says *yes*, then we can say, "The entire trauma that I experienced in my past life under the Inquisition, I now give you permission to start the self-healing process." Once that's being said, these traumatic experiences are being released or healed. Effective use of SID can be as simple as that, and from there, we can go to deeper layers, and bring healing to all aspects of our being.

If you just ask my current life and past lives to start the self-healing process, it's going to work but it's going to go a little slower. It's going to work on the full spectrum level without knowing specifics. That's why it is important to have key points to expedite the transformational process. You can benefit from a SID practitioner who can support you in finding those key points. You can go into the specifics of a past life without getting lost because your practitioner is going with you. If you were by yourself, your system could say, " This is to traumatic. We can get back to this point later."—Or we can do it right now, with a practitioner, and you can trust that you will be fine. You can clear the past life, in which the energy is still stuck from a traumatic experience, and call your power back to you. In the media room where all these screens are running a multitude of movies at the same time, you can choose the one scene in the one movie that you want to transform and with surgical precision we will change the event without leaving you traumatized. You're actually calling your power back to yourself and you prevail.

During SID, we're dealing with a full spectrum life experience cycle, which plays a big role. There are many dimensions to the depth of human existence. It's not just one-dimensional, it's multidimensional. As you go deeper, you have different experiential levels. When we start with Sacred Inner Dialogue, we start on the surface as to establish first what's going on, and we say, "I'm working on this repeating issue over and over to reach all of its levels." And that's something we can indeed successfully accomplish.

Imagine how hard it must be if you were a queen in a past life, but now have to live an ordinary life and do the things your servants once did for you. You might feel demoted, or resentful that life is forcing you to do something you don't think you signed up for, and you constantly repeat experiences of resentment.

Being in different roles at different times and accepting where and who we are today is so important. Acknowledging is so important. Transforming is so important. When we go into a past life and we have a memory of being a king, and we are suppressed all the time in this lifetime, we keep wondering, "What's going on?" We want to get out of this lifetime and get back to our other lifetime, and that's obviously not going to work. That's what happens when people forget to approach this lifetime as an opportunity to fill in the blanks. There are past lives when we've had amazing lifetimes and past lives we didn't consider so amazing and we wonder why we had to suffer.

What's going on is that we are filling in an "experience wheel." We are beings who are experiencing and integrating experiences, and that's where a big part of our learning originates. Whether we deem them pleasant or unpleasant, these are all great experiences that gave us insights and ultimately created a full spectrum of who we are today. Instead of seeing them as a hindrance or blockage, let us acknowledge that we are given through them an opportunity to see life from a different perspective. It's nothing different from an actor or an actress who does not wish to be stuck with only one or two roles. After a while you say, "I can play about any role."

> *The more versatile you can become, the more of a*
> *full spectrum person you become, and the more you*
> *tap into your full spectrum of light and potential.*

That's the same as experiencing ever more lifetimes. We are experiencing what we are experiencing so that we can become more effective. The more we can recognize and focus on our main soul purpose, the more we can specialize in these fields.

In my case, a lot of people say, "You have so much wisdom that you can tap into it." When I look at it, I see that I had already access to a lot of wisdom when I came to this planet. A lot of my present wisdom is what I implemented from past lives. Yet, regardless of past and present wisdom, I and you can still specialize because life is unlimited. You can still go deeper in your healing if that's your passion and your soul's purpose.

I supported throughout different lifetimes civilizations on their path to become more effective as an advanced civilization. What does a civilization need? What infrastructure is required? I was bringing in and deliberating on that infrastructure in many lifetimes, and that's what comes easily to me today: how to arrange and to make energy substructures visible in a person's life and streamline them. Everyone has their own cycles and experiences to go through for various reasons.

A memory is being memorized in your system and that's why we have certain ailments, experiences or limitations. Is that going to define you? I don't think so. You have a chance to work on ailments, experiences and limitations as you encounter them. SID is as if you were watching a documentary or movie of your inner world. Besides having a visceral experience, you're feeling the full firsthand experience of it. Sacred Inner Dialogue gives you a very deep access to your past, current, future and parallel lives.

D. ENLIGHTENMENT THROUGH SERVICE

When Buddha came into existence 2,500 years ago, he remembers being a white elephant. He has many lifetimes, of which he recalls coming into this world as a white elephant or another being.

Buddha spoke about the more than five hundred lifetimes that he had lived. Five hundred might seem a high number, yet it would be more appropriate to see those lifetimes in the context of many thousands of lifetimes and eons of life cycles, since we know that life didn't just start six thousand years ago. Evolution has seen mineral and organic lives developing—being reborn into—ever more complex life forms, so that we are truly talking about eons of cycles of time and life. Each of Buddha's lifetimes means a thousand Buddha lives, and every past life was a whole cycle. Buddha has so many lifetimes. If we acknowledge having ten lifetimes or thousands and eons of lifetimes, we can say that in ten lifetimes we have ten full cycles memorized.

One of Buddha's stories is recalled in the Shakyamuni Buddha, where Buddha is a rich Brahman named Sumedha. While being in full incarnation in one of the stupas (a place of meditation), he realizes that life is characterized by suffering, and he chooses to go beyond what he had seen so far and to seek Enlightenment by becoming a hermit and living in a cave. Upon seeing the Buddha for the first time, Sumedha is in awe and puts his long black hair down for the Buddha to step on so that he could cross a puddle of mud without soiling his feet. This is just one of many of Buddha's stories how he came to Enlightenment.

Buddha served on the path to his own Enlightenment.

One of the most momentous reasons explaining why service or healing work is so important is because you can get to your own personal Enlightenment. When we are looking at Mother Teresa or Jesus serving sick people, we see a form of service. Through your enlightened service, you pave your way to your own Enlightenment because you understand that serving yourself and Oneness is everything. Supporting the healing of others and assisting ourselves in our self-healing is such service that will advance you on your personal path to Enlightenment. Through healing you can get to your own Enlightenment, even if you don't feel as if you would have the qualifications, so-to-speak.

Service can happen in so many different ways. SID is one powerful way to serve yourself and others. By using SID, you can gain understanding of your past lifetimes; you understand that through our past lifetimes we are going into cycles of experiences that allow us to gain full spectrum insight into all facets of what it means to be human. A lot of people do not yet fully understand the levels of past lives and their significance for their present existence and their development. Jesus was one of those who understood. Until the belief in reincarnation was suppressed by the early Church from the 6th century after Christ on, there existed amazing stories of even Jesus talking about past lives.

6. LIST OF TOPICS AND AREAS IN OUR LIVES THAT WE CAN IMPROVE THROUGH SACRED INNER DIALOGUE

A Sacred Inner Dialogue can be about any aspect of our lives. It is a tool to communicate with your higher Self, with your inner divine self, with the seat of all knowledge, and it is also a means of connecting to All-Oneness. The possibilities of its use are infinite. In the following, I wish to show you a listing of some of the topics and areas in our lives that can be greatly improved and supported through SID.

These topics and areas can benefit us the most in creating a healthy life that we enjoy living and that is filled with those experiences we truly desire:

- Excellent Health
- Soul-Satisfying Prosperity
- Prosperity
- Higher Levels of Abundance
- Higher Levels of Money
- Higher Levels of Time
- Higher Levels of Space

- Higher Levels of Love
- Higher Levels of Psychic Abilities
- Higher Levels of Metaphysical Understanding
- Higher Levels of Healing Abilities
- Higher Levels of Star Family Connections
- Higher Levels of Energy
- Higher Levels of Emotional Fulfillment
- Higher Levels of Spiritual Fulfillment
- Higher Levels of Physical Fulfillment
- Higher Levels of Mental Fulfillment
- Spiritual Healing
- Transforming Poverty to Abundance
- Transforming Hopelessness to Hope
- Transforming Unhealthy Relationships to Soul-Fulfilling Connections
- Transforming the Impossible to Possible
- Transforming Unhealthy Nutrition Patterns to Healthy Nourishment Habits
- Transforming the Feeling of Being Stuck
- Transforming Depression
- Transforming Procrastination
- Stepping into One's Purpose
- Creating Healthier Boundaries with Family and Finding Your Tribe
- Letting Go of What No Longer Serves Our Soul

- Letting Go of the Past and Traumatic Experiences
- Becoming Aware of Being in Denial and Stepping into Healing
- Moving Forward
- Transforming Disconnectedness to Full Connectedness with Life
- Creating a Sense of Belonging and Fitting In
- Entity Release
- Removal of Implants
- Removal of Unhealthy Attachments

A. APPROACHES FOR SACRED INNER DIALOGUES

There are many ways of conducting Sacred Inner Dialogues. Here are some tested formulas for effective work with SID:

Start out by naming whatever you wish to work with, i.e., "My soul-satisfying prosperity."

"My soul-satisfying prosperity, can you hear me?"

Once it answers, we can ask it:

"My soul-satisfying prosperity, please become fully present now."

The next example addresses the experience of not being in healthy alignment with our service in life:

"Any unhealthy patterns of misaligned service from my lineage affecting me, can you hear me?"

Once it answers, we can ask it:

"Unhealthy patterns of misaligned service from my lineage affecting me, please start the transformational process and give me more space."

Then we move to addressing misguided belief systems by following this example here. Know that "better" or "healthier" represents many things such as more money, perfect health, a better house, better appliances, a nicer car, more space, more time:

"My belief system in which better is not available for me, can you hear me?"

Once it answers with "Yes," then we ask it to be transformed and replaced with a healthier belief system:

"My belief system in which better is not available for me, it is time for you to be transformed and replaced with a healthier belief system. The new healthier belief system is: Better and healthier is available for me at all times."

In this situation, as well as in general with SID, please utilize the duality aspect of the positive and negative, of yin and yang, for solution finding and key insights. For example, here we went from the belief system that better is not available to us to "Better and healthier is available for me at all times," resulting in the exact opposite.

Observe here, often I use "please start the transformational process" and often I address it directly, the choice of which depends on the willingness of the issues to want to start the transformational process.

Returning to our SID, we now ask the cause of our belief system in which better is not available for me:

"Cause of the belief system that better is not available for me, can you hear me?"

As soon as it answers "Yes," we ask:

"Cause of the belief system in which better is not available for me, please start the transformational healing process."

Employing SID prior to surgeries is also a great support for you.

Now ask:

"My higher self, can you hear me?"

Once it answers "Yes," then ask:

"My higher self, please coordinate my surgery and organize my recovery in the best way possible."

If you are the person performing the surgery, say:

"My higher self, can you hear me?"

Once it answers "Yes," ask:

"My higher self, please coordinate the successful surgery."

Use a more individualized form of SID to increase self-love and the feeling of self-worth whenever you experience negative programs running on your inner hard drive, or when someone is projecting negativity at you. I would like us to use the program of increasing self-love and the feeling of self-worth to love ourselves stronger than people hate us. So we can stay in the power of self-love and motivate us in our self-healing through it.

"My self-love, can you hear me?"

Once it answers "Yes," we ask our self-love:

"My self-love, please raise yourself to the highest level possible and infuse all of my being."

Now we move on to our compromised self-worth:

"My compromised self-worth, can you hear me?"

Once it answers "Yes," we ask:

"My compromised self-worth, please start the transformational healing process."

Then we ask:

"My self-worth, can you hear me?"

Once it answers "Yes," we say:

"My self-worth, raise yourself to the highest level possible."

Here are some more topics to work on transforming using the before mentioned script:

"My Compromised Inner Child, can you hear me?"

"My Compromised Immune System, can you hear me?"

"My Compromised Authentic Self, can you hear me?"

"My Compromised Success, can you hear me?"

"My Compromised Liberty from Organized Religion, can you hear me?"

"My Compromised Self-approval, can you hear me?"

"My Compromised Energy Field, can you hear me?"

"Increase of Confidence and "Confidancing" (dancing with confidence), can you hear me?"

Here is a script to transform negative projections from your enemies:

"I love myself more than my enemies hate me" (knowing that they ultimately hate themselves). You can transform any self-hatred in the same manner.

The key to a successful Sacred Inner Dialogue is to *acknowledge* what there is that needs to be addressed, to *appreciate* it, then lovingly ask it to *transform*.

Acknowledge with words, and also with your inner intention, what you hold towards the issue that needs to be addressed. Appreciate it (whatever "it" is), even though you might perceive it as a problem currently, because it is there for a reason (remember what we discovered in that respect earlier about "fear"). Finally, command its transformation firmly yet with loving-kindness. Through SID, you are taking command of your life. You set the terms for your health and wellbeing on all levels of your existence. Therefore, your grace, you don't have to beg because you have the power and duty to command, like a Queen or a King, with honor and with grace.

Whenever you feel unsure as to which direction your Sacred Inner Dialogue should take, surrender to the stream of your consciousness, and allow yourself to be guided by your inner wisdom.

Use the following phrases as you feel guided:

"My higher self, can you hear me?"

"God/Goddess, can you hear me?"

"Jesus, can you hear me?"

"Healing angels, can you hear me?"

"Universe, can you hear me?"

"My Enlightenment, can you hear me?"

"Multiversal father energy, can you hear me?"

"Multiversal mother energy, can you hear me?"

"Me owning and expressing my full potential, can you hear me?"

"Everything that's blocking me to stay healthy, can you hear me? Everything blocking me to stay healthy, I now give you permission to transform."

7. LIVING YOUR PURPOSE AND RECEIVING PROSPERITY

Living and serving your purpose leads automatically to more income and prosperity.

In order for us to bring in and activate the right energy to become receptive for prosperity, we have to look at lack consciousness and transform it. Why is there a belief of lack of time, space, friendship, or money, and why is that frequency still in our system? That has to be addressed in order for it to be transformed and replaced with a healthier, more abundant belief system and corresponding experiences.

Lack can manifest in many forms. Often it manifests in our job or through other activities we engage in or "have to do", and we can recognize whether we are in a space of abundance or lack by thinking about the following: In some instances, it doesn't matter how much time you're dedicating to an activity because you love what you're doing, and when you don't love something that you're doing, then you're counting every hour. That's lack. Whenever you do something that is burdensome and exhausting and no fun, you are experiencing lack. When you're doing something and it's a loving joy, you want to go deeper into it. That's abundance. When you understand that, you get to a place where whatever you want to do and love to do becomes an effortless manifestation of progress.

We dedicate time, we dedicate space, and we dedicate energy to a certain project because we love what we do. That is the foundation for success.

Success and career is paired with loving what we do. When we are talking about it, we are looking at how many times we're doing something we didn't love to do. We have to look at finding something we love to do that doesn't require us to look at it as work, but rather like a hobby. That's why so many people start in their later years with performing music or painting or doing something else that's highly creative. They start doing it because that's what they always wanted to do. Some start very late to turn to music, painting, energy work or something else, and find the new activity highly enjoyable and some of them become really successful. A lot of people change what they do in life to what they really want to do, and that's when they reap the greatest success in their lives. A lot of people love their hobby and turn it into a profession because that is what they love to do and their passion automatically takes over. Somebody, for example, collects coins or stamps he or she starts to trade them and makes a living with it. Another person likes to cook, all of a sudden starts cooking for friends and is being asked to cater for entire parties.

Some people love to do healing work. Some people love to write, so they become writers. We have to bring that love and focus of loving into everything that we do so that it can become prosperous, and be fueled with the energy of prosperity and effortlessness. That's a big part of it. How do we change what we are doing? At a later point in life, for instance, a lot of people wish to become Energy healers. How about that sudden urge, where is it coming from? I know people from all walks of life who say, "I'm ready to be an Energy healer," You wonder how in the world they came from being an accountant or any profession to suddenly wanting to be a healer. Typically, the answer is, "I feel my calling, I want to be a healer." They change their profession to become an energy healer, massage therapist, nurse, or they take up another healing profession. What a noble and compassionate intention.

Instead of self-serving they're starting to serve humanity, animals or want to plant trees to support the environment and Mother Earth and the overall raising of consciousness.

A. CREATING SPACE

Even though it is by living our purpose that we receive most prosperity, we are often afraid to make what might seem to be a radical change in our professional lives. We face fear or anxiety of not having enough. That fear stems from lack consciousness.

When we desire major changes in our lives, we are often being challenged by the universe. It is as if we'd awoken all kinds of sleeping dogs and we are suddenly challenged to demonstrate whether we are serious about our desires through stumble stones on our paths. Addictions are one type of these stumble stones. When people want to transform stress in their lives (which is another form of lack since we believe in that moment we are not enough), they typically feel overwhelmed by the thought of letting go of past habits or addictions in any form such as alcohol, food, sex, or gambling.

When people decide to let go of addictions, it's important for them to utilize the Sacred Inner Dialogues, because that is already the first step towards achieving success even when they still feel like being in the grip of their addiction. They start communicating and educating themselves rather than being victims of their inner voice that tells them they have to consume a specific substance or engage in a certain action. With SID, we start by simply saying to the addiction, "Just give me a little bit more space."

When we talk about having more space, it's not for pressuring you or pushing you to do anything right now, it simply gives you more choices. If you have to do something right now, then you do not have space—you cannot ask a question—and are most likely being suppressed, or feeling smothered by the issue.

Just one sentence, "Hi there, my addiction, please give me more space" is more than enough to address the addiction. It doesn't have to be *transformed* and *be gone*—just ask it gently for a little bit more space.

SID is created to create sacred inner space. The more inner space we have, the more we can expand our consciousness into this life. The less space we have, the less we can be present, because our habits, our addictions, our programming from past lives and from our lineage, and our belief system from growing up are all active in our minds, in our hearts, in our bodies, in our entire system. If we ask for more space, we can bring in more consciousness. When we have more consciousness, we can express more of who we really are instead of just functioning on autopilot and expressing ourselves in automated ways that are not even a reflection of who we really are. That's why Sacred Inner Dialogue is so important: It creates space for us. Once we have space, we can start to utilize this space, harness it, and fill it with something that's strengthening us.

Instead of the addiction, we can now bring in healthier habits of eating, sleeping, and thinking.

B. DETOXING

When people come to me and they want to detox, there are so many levels of toxins in the system that we have to look at, including emotional toxins, mental toxins, spiritual toxins and physical toxins. The last extent of inner toxicity is physical, so the body gets toxic, too. All of these are interrelated. It's good to have a footbath to physically detox but people have to go through detox on all levels because they are constantly exposed to negativity and toxicity. It is important for them to start cultivating healthy emotions and belief systems on the levels required for a healthy life.

When you work with Sacred Inner Dialogue you can ask these toxins to start the releasing process, or you can say, "Give me more space." You can also ask, "Toxins in my system, can you hear me?"

See if you receive a response in form of an energy sensation, physical goosebumps, whether you hear a "Yes" or "No," or see a color in front of your eyes. Any response is important to acknowledge. Also, don't question yourself and think, "Am I just thinking this or is this really happening?" Relax and trust in yourself. Instead of doubting whether something is happening, take it for what it is, and acknowledge the sensation you received as a genuine response. Once the toxins respond, ask them to give you more space, if you don't know yet what to do next. At least you now have more space and are not crowded with toxins, and this will allow you to be able to reflect and decide on the next step with more ease.

After creating more inner space, you can start utilizing your inner system.

Now you are ready to say, "Whatever I can do to support the detoxification of my system, I now invite this in: "Healthy detox, can you hear me?" Then we ask the healthy detox to enter the toxic space, or the toxins, and to release them gracefully.

You can also talk to the toxins directly, "My mental toxicity, can you hear me?" Or: "My toxic thoughts, can you hear me?" Soon you will hear the toxic thoughts saying, "Yes, I can hear you." When the toxic thoughts can hear you, you say, "Toxic thoughts, please give me more space so I can implement healthy thought patterns."

Then the toxic thoughts say, "OK". —Why do they say OK? Because everything in your system is smaller than The System. Your life is bigger than any of this. Your life is the house these toxic thoughts live in. Without you, they are not there. They want to make sure to work with you, otherwise, you are just going to get rid of them. That's why they are going to cooperate sooner or later. In the beginning they may not cooperate because they might be thinking, "I'm more powerful than you because you gave me a lot of power." When you start calling your power back, they will realize they are smaller than you are and start to cooperate.

Know: It's a mirage. They cannot be bigger than you because they are smaller than you, that's why they are in you. They wouldn't need you if they were bigger than you. They would go and just be living by themselves. They will eventually cooperate, and once you understand that, you can start harnessing the richness of your inner world. It becomes a sacred inner world followed by sacred inner space, which becomes a sacred inner life that turns into a sacred outer life.

That's something that you want to observe and then harness.

"Gentle detox, can you hear me?" Then ask that gentle detox, "Flow into all aspects of my toxicity." Then you have already put it into motion, gently, without having to go through a healing crisis all the time for everything. You can just slowly detox.

In a like manner, you can effect changes towards more healthful nutrition.

Remember, detoxing and changing habits is a fun tug of war game measured in inches, inch-by-inch-by inch, until you take your life back.

As a practitioner, I have encountered people whose systems are so crowded by unhealthy behavioral patterns and beliefs that I talked to them about their personal inner dialogue for years. I assist them in guided Sacred Inner Dialogues, until one day, they all of a sudden do it themselves. They come to me and say, "When I felt anxiety coming on, I just asked it for a little bit more space and it worked!"

It's not just about space and being less crowded, this is about putting solutions into place to fill the empty space with information, programs, patterns, thoughts and energies that are more useful for a person than the prior toxic material.

C. CLEANSING AND CLEARING

There's so much sophistication going on in our system. Sacred Inner Dialogue allows us to cleanse and clear innumerable aspects of our being and our existence. Here are a few more examples to illustrate the breadth of its possible uses.

If you look at entities, for example, and go into clearing yourself from past relationships or past life attachments, you're going into a place where you have the opportunity to start an inner dialogue with the entities or with people who passed over. You can start the dialogue at any moment, even if you didn't have a chance to release somebody in the physical world. You can ask them in their state of passing over if they can hear you, and if there's anything you can do for them. Most of the time, I recommend to burn a candle for them when people pass over, so they can be connected with the light. Then I suggest to ask them, if they can support you to release whatever attachment or trauma links you to them, so that you can freely move forward in your life:

"Any entities that are draining my life force, can you hear me?"

Once they say "Yes," ask them:

"Any entities that are draining my life force, give me more space and return my life force."

This is part of the healing being done with Sacred Inner Dialogue.

When it comes to success, call in the energy of success to create success. If you are trying to do something and you are constantly failing, then ask the energy of failure to give you more space so you can introduce the energy of success.

If you are foggy in your mind, then ask the fogginess for more space so you can introduce more clarity into your life.

If you feel drained or exhausted, then ask the exhaustion to give you more space so you can start recharging and having your energy back and having your energy available to start doing the things you wish to accomplish.

If you suffer from chronic fatigue, and feel totally fatigued all the time, then that's a pattern that you can address with SID. Ask the energy of fatigue to give you more space so you can fully recharge and have more energy and life force.

D. OUR LIFE FORCE

As a practitioner, a lot of what I do with Sacred Inner Dialogue is supporting people to become more fully present in their lives. It is a common phenomenon that people literally "check out" when things get really challenging in their lives. Most prominently so when people reach a point at which they don't want to live anymore. Even if they might make it through the worst of this challenging experience, their energy remains compromised. Their life force became less and less available to them as they grow older. Their system is noticeably depleted of life force, and they are not fully present in their lives.

Through SID, we ask the life force outside of their bodies, my life force that is not currently accessible to me, if it can hear me. Once this life force says "Yes," we ask it to fully return into this body, into this current life, so that we can be our fully recharged selves and be able to attract whatever we need to attract to live our purpose. Life force is the source that attracts everything into our lives because life force is magnetic. The more life force is in our bodies, the less we have to do because it attracts whatever we need, like a magnet. When we checked out or committed suicide in any of our past lives, our present life will be characterized by a compromised life force. We need to call our life force back to us, so it can become available for us, so we can start living all aspects of our lives fully.

It's important that we get our power and life force back without feeling that we have to give our energy away to others, but feeling good about keeping our energy for ourselves. Then we can attract more and more opportunities. This is by no means selfish. A big part of realizing this is teaching how to keep our life force but sending our unconditional love to the people dear to us. What drains us is sending our own life force to someone else. Unconditional love is the highest energy we can send and it is the highest gift to receive.

Everyone is after love and love is the highest frequency.

A lot of people deny themselves in order to be loved. When you get into an understanding that sending unconditional love is the same as sending the freely available energy of unconditional love that is in existence, you will never deplete yourself. Rather than draining your own life force and giving personal energy to your parents and family members, you can send the freely available, infinite energy of unconditional love. I'm using the example of giving your energy to parents and family members because ninety-nine percent of us give our parents our life force as children. This creates more energy in them so they can make more money to support us and put a roof above our heads, feed us and take care of the family needs. When that happens, we are conditioned to give our energy away in exchange of them providing for us. That pattern is still active when we leave the house of our parents. However, if we don't collectively change this pattern, we're still giving away our energy to parents and family members instead of unconditional love. When we live our life moving forward, we're still doing the same thing. We're giving away our life force and that depletes us.

Some people out there will take your life force without blinking an eye. They wouldn't even feel bad about it. What's important is to change that pattern in our digestive system or solar plexus chakra and unhook the faucets and hoses installed by family members and people close to us.

When we're feeling that deficiency we have to shift it to unconditional love. When we shift it to unconditional love, we cannot be depleted because there's enough of it in us and in the Universe. Unconditional love is the substance which we are made of. Drawing from it, we are not getting exhausted.

I call all of my life force back to me to stay with me.

I now send unconditional love into all aspects of this multiverse including myself.

8. WORKING WITH SACRED INNER DIALOGUE

First we want to know what the person wishes to work on. As a practitioner, I energetically tune in on my client, then I utilize Sacred Inner Dialogue and create sacred space to check and balance each chakra, which represents a certain area. This allows me to tune into the energetic needs of a person.

If you want to go deeper into energy work itself, I recommend you to read my book the Ataanamethod.

A. THE IMPORTANCE OF ROOT AND CROWN CHAKRA

The first chakra is relevant to our Mother Earth connection. Whenever you don't flow well in your first chakra, then it's due to an issue related to mother problems, roughly speaking. Our physical energy system needs to be grounded and connected with Mother Earth because any overload we have in our system, can then dispel to and through our first chakra. The key here is to see why the system is not grounded. We then ground our system and implement a better software on the computer. Once the computer is grounded it is able to achieve a better long-term performance.

When someone says they are not grounded, it gives me a clear signal that there is something going on between that person and their mother. When we have something going on with our mother that gives us an interference with Mother Earth because our mother is our closest connection to Mother Earth. Even if any abuse took place, we would have expected our mother to protect us.

Parents do what they can do. Sometimes it's excellent. Sometimes it's not enough. What matters is that it affects our first chakra. The feeling we have of feeling disconnected with our mother is the same feeling on the earth, in our work, in our life. It transferred from our mother to the next bigger mother, which is Mother Earth. Then the next bigger mother is the Mother Divine, Mother Mary, or the Goddess.

That's the disconnectedness that we will then transfer to the next bigger issue because that's our experience. The subconscious program is that Mother Earth is the same as our own mother. If we have imbalances in our first chakra, we are conditioned to believe that she is not going to show up when we need Her. Our system thinks, "It's a repeating pattern. Mother Earth acts the same way as my own mother." One way or another we're drawing the conclusion, "If my mother is this way, so are the rest of the females on the planet. Getting along with the females is not going to be easy because they just take, don't give enough, or are not present."

However, our biological mother or mother figure who raises us has nothing to do with Mother Earth in the sense that she didn't show up for us. Mother Earth guides every step we take because Mother Earth is right underneath our feet. She supports and carries us, including our biological mother.

Another key check besides the first chakra, is checking how well the seventh chakra flows. The seventh chakra is our male connection to God. If the seventh chakra is not flowing, there's a male-related problem.

We can easily detect whether there's a deficiency in the chakra by putting our hands on the crown chakra. I can tell where there is a deficiency in the energy field and work through what the chakras represent to guide you through the healing process. The same mechanism works for any other chakra.

The root and crown chakra are of eminent importance. We can't say one is the highest and the other is the lowest because some say there are other chakras above the head and underneath our root chakra. The first chakra and seventh chakra are simple access points to our energy system. We can tell if there are deficiencies and approach these deficiencies very easily through the first and seventh chakra. This is where we start our energetic mapping.

Let's say we discover a deficiency in the root chakra. We ask, "What happened between you and your mother?" "Were you not breastfed? Were you abandoned? Neglected?" When the first chakra doesn't feel connected to earth, that's a sign of separation. It's the same with the crown chakra. We ask, "Do you feel emotionally rejected from your father?" If he was unavailable, that's an absence, a form of rejection, abandonment at the core, feeling separated, undernourished, and unsupported. Disconnection in either of these two chakras needs to be mended. To live a healthy life, we need to be reconnected to these two principal, life-giving sources.

The father and the mother here on earth are smaller representatives of the Greater God and Goddess Mother Earth. If we have a conflict with our mother or father, we're projecting this onto our main Male, Female Source. It means we are harboring separation.

When that happens, it's a deficiency. We are automatically agreeing to the deficiency of feeling malnourished, rejected and abandoned and feel God is doing the same thing to us. Our parents abandoned us and we are tempted to think the same thing about God or our Source because of our experience, and the subconscious projects this to the next higher level. It's like having a diplomat in your country and that diplomat in the country doesn't want to talk to you, and you automatically think the President doesn't want to talk to you either.

Everyone is a diplomat and everyone is a reflection of the infinite. The next higher part is a connection to infinity, and the subconscious puts a blocking pattern on it, where you block the bigger picture. Your subconscious does it automatically because it doesn't think in terms of higher levels of wholeness. It sees what has happened and remains in limitation instead of unlimitedness. That's why it is so important to consciously connect yourself to the higher level.

When we give energy to the deficient chakras
and balance them, then we are ready to go
deeper into Sacred Inner Dialogue.

B. ACKNOWLEDGMENT AND UNCONDITIONAL LOVE

If something is not acknowledged, it doesn't matter how many times it is being communicated, a dozen or million times, communicating the pattern doesn't change it—it actually reinforces the pattern. If you don't acknowledge it, it doesn't mean anything. That's why people repeat patterns. You are still fostering a pattern from childhood, and it is not being acknowledged. It's being repeated at this moment with people and you don't know why. It's as simple as going back to the moment when it was created and acknowledging it. As long as it is not acknowledged, that pattern still runs uncontrollably.

When I say acknowledge, you have to ask me, "How do I acknowledge?" That is very significant because you can acknowledge something, *acknowledge something*, or truly **acknowledge something**. It's not me acknowledging it, it's not the outside world acknowledging it, it is when you acknowledge something that's happening inside of you, right? Some patterns you can acknowledge, and "poof," they are gone. Some patterns require you to really understand them in their full complexity. Was it a past life experience? Did the pattern start in this life? Does it stem from childhood? When was the exact moment? A lot of people already know they had, for example, a traumatic experience of sexual or verbal or emotional abuse, let's say, at the age of seven. We can then directly travel back to that moment in time.

I like these types of consultations because you already know what you want to work on. You say, "I want to work on this abuse pattern," or, "I want to change my approach of how I want to do something." As the practitioner, I ask, "When did you start doing it this way?" So far, we have been experiencing patterns of suppression. No one in your life has ever been truly interested in knowing what's happening with you. Your patterns are more interested in not being acknowledged. Sometimes it is not easy to remember and even to repeat the words since the patterns try to protect themselves. We are changing the neurons and are laying new pathways in your brain. That's why it is sometimes better to repeat the proclamations several times. And by us truly saying these words, we are acknowledging and accepting these new pathways. There are infinite definitions of acknowledgment. Everyone's definition of acknowledgement is different—this is why it's important that you, not me, fully acknowledge your pattern. True healing happens as the acknowledgment happens. You are actually confronted with the life energy of the event, with the core dynamic that was present at the creation of this pattern. That's as traumatic and as intense as it was when you were right in that moment when it actually happened, but you know now that you are safe because I'm right there with you.

That's why you can go deeper in a Sacred Inner Dialogue that you engage in under professional guidance. That's also how you are able to acknowledge at the same time the pattern in its full energetic presence. I'm there supporting you to redirect that energy in a healthy way. That's what makes the difference. To a certain extent it is my acknowledgment as well, and through my connectedness to the Oneness, all of existence is witnessing what's happening and more importantly than anything else, you are actually acknowledging what's happening without feeling you have to suppress the experience.

Have you heard the saying, sunlight is the best disinfectant by Louis Brandeis? If not, you have heard it now. Once you bring any experience up to the surface, it is already part of the transformational process. It occupies space. Little roots go all over the place because it finds perfect soil in our subconscious. With SID, we are really diving into the subconscious, into the fertile ground of our inner existence, and here we are deciding which plants are healthy for us and which ones are not. From there, we can break through to the super conscious, to all the multi-dimensionality of existence. But it really starts in the subconscious, that's where the seedling breaks through the soil, and by watching the sprout, we see how big its potential for growth is there. Then we can say, "Hey, I want that space in there to plant a good seed instead of a traumatic seed."

After the acknowledgment and observing the full extent of the depth, we can see whether we really are in the Oneness. If you are not, you see dualities as good or bad. The Oneness is an acceptance of a phenomenon beyond its appearance. In Oneness, you don't judge if it's good or bad because it's energy. Some duality is necessary. We are not so much judging or condemning the duality as we are allowing it to support the Oneness. It's almost like playing a piano. If you play a piano, you have the black and the white keys. The different notes grounded in duality create this Oneness song. That's how we are creating Oneness.

> *Duality is being in the conflict stage.*
> *From the place of Oneness, that*
> *conflict is already resolved.*

There is also an interesting connection between SID and sound healing:

The frequency of addressing an issue and communicating, resetting and replacing a dysfunctional pattern with a healthy program, rewires the neurons of the brain. In order to gauge the moment of this rewiring, I often let the clients repeat the SID protocol until I feel the sound frequency is aligned. I highly recommend to look into sound healing and cymascope to learn about the fascinating structure of sound.

Please look up and practice my <u>Prosperity Healing Mantras</u> on iTunes to gain deeper insight.

I come from a place where this whole thing is already resolved. I do not focus too much on duality. When you speak about duality, don't be afraid because it's an aspect of the overall Oneness. Duality explains Oneness, but not sufficiently (because the explanation is tainted by the illusion of separation between these two sides). In Oneness, everything is and is not. It's not a shortcut or illusion. Understanding these concepts is the avenue to utilize the full potential for acknowledgment. When I say acknowledge, I mean loving everything unconditionally. Understanding the word "acknowledge," and following this approach, is an important ingredient to self-healing. If you do not love yourself and all of life unconditionally, it does no good to desire to be somewhere else because the lack of love would follow you there. The first priority is to activate the unconditional love within your heart. Unconditional love is a good measuring device to see where you are in your life. You'll go from "Look at how dysfunctional human beings are" into the unconditional love of Oneness, and say, "Everything has the right to be, even the worst patterns, otherwise why would they be there? Also, why would you bask in the experience that you don't love when you could instead create everything you wish for in this Multiverse?" In the Oneness, all can be. Now choose what you wish for yourself.

This is what makes SID so effective:
Acknowledgment and unconditional love.

The Beatles song *All You Need is Love* reflects back to us a foundational principle of life itself: Our love is the main ingredient for creation and transformation. All ingredients are in the heart. This tool is so effective because it is activated through acknowledgement and unconditional love is the frequency required to change anything we desire to change.

You created something because you love it, otherwise why would you create it? Love and hate are really close and both are very powerful energies. When you hate something you have a very intense disharmonious energy. When you apply it to sound level, you could compare hate to chaotic disorganized noise versus love to harmonious healing sounds. Certain love harmonies are required to create a pattern because a pattern just doesn't happen on its own. These patterns are formed by energy and sound, as the impressive work by Masaru Emoto on the formation of water crystals so clearly illustrates. We are made of approximately sixty percent of water, and our reactions to energies are quite alike to the reaction of water crystals, or even that of quartz crystals made up of silica, which is in itself a material found in the human body and needed for the preservation of its functions and youthfulness. Trauma or a harmonious pattern happens by certain actions that lead to us either into high frequency stress or into high frequency ecstatic situations. The experiences you have are recorded by the brain or muscle memory, and these memories become embedded in the system.

Before they show up in the brain system or muscle memory system, experiences are in your energy memory system. That means that your non-physical self holds recorded the intense energy of traumatic experiences from past lives, in which you might have died on the battlefield. Your Self recorded the energy of these disharmonious traumatic experiences like a sound recorder, like a black box from a plane. These experiences are picked up on by a microphone that record all levels of noise. Upon our next incarnation, these patterns are impressed on our body, mind and spirit. They often make themselves visible as moles, irregularities and behavioral patterns. Moles often mark the place where we had been shot or severely injured in a past life.

You take that recorded memory with you and create a similar experience, maybe not as strong because it was so far away and the recording fades, but similar to it. Then it depends on your awareness to recognize the pattern and change it. Once you know you have a traumatic experience that you carry with you, you have the opportunity (and duty toward yourself) to start working on it. If you are a person who died on the battlefield or have posttraumatic stress disorder, it's about understanding the conflict, finding forgiveness and transforming the traumatic death experience.

Seeing it in the energy system and traveling back to the source is what allows me to fully observe the pattern and support you to rewrite it through SID.

This is why this modality is so effective, because you don't need to torment yourself for hours to relive a traumatic experience. You can automatically express it. You don't have to jump through hoops to get there. Requirements are: awareness and willingness.

It's almost like you are handed a key that allows you to go back to that moment or situation and enables you to say, "It doesn't matter what you're showing me, I'm not resenting it. I love it." All the negative patterns that come up in your mind, you're not resenting them, and that means you're not filtering them too much. This method is so effective that it can open the floodgate to radical transformation, or as I like to call it now: graceful *transformation*.

With this map, I can guide you to past lives and any other places to support you in recognizing and changing a pattern within comparatively little time, and to enable you to live your most effective life.

C. ENERGY WORK

The ultimate expression of self-love is doing energy work on yourself. When you do energy work on yourself you are healing yourself.

If you were a ghost without a body, you'd say, "Person in a body, can you do this for me? That would be great."

When you get into a place where you have a body, you ultimately declare that you want to participate in life. When you show the Universe and Multiverse, God, and all divine energies that you love being here, that's when you start doing something positive with your body in this life.

This is the moment when you say, "I want to serve. I want to do this, I want to do that," and you receive support from the Universe.

But when you hear someone say, "I don't want to do this. I hate this. Ugh, bah, this could be better", it means somebody doesn't really want to be here. That is not an attitude of gratitude. It is an attitude of being fed up with something instead of appreciating every second of our experience on this planet. When we are in this space of lacking appreciation for our lives, that's where we have to improve and approve of ourselves. That's when we need to get to a place where we can say, "I fully appreciate myself and my life, and I fully approve of myself and my life."

How can you say this with conviction? Only when you know you are doing the right thing. If you are not doing what you recognize as right, you cannot fully approve of yourself. Of course, that gives you motivation to do the right thing. Even if you have not always done the right thing so far, you came into this world fully equipped for doing the right thing—whatever that service, your purpose, your personal "right thing" might be.

You can always find and refine your purpose. It will not get lost. You can always realign yourself with your purpose, you can do it in this moment, immediately, and you will experience immediate results.

The tool for doing so—the Sacred Inner Dialogue—is such a strong, transformational tool that it will automatically help you to deal with any issues and question that might come up, as long as you keep the momentum going and are sincere in its application.

It is important to note that the Ataana Method combined with SID as a tool for healing and self-healing will result in an experience as unique and individual as every individual life on this planet is in itself. Everyone is going to respond differently to transformational work. If you have already been working in the field for some time, a lot of what you are going to encounter might resonate with experiences you had before. If you are just starting out in the field of energy work, your experience might be unlike anything you've ever experienced in this lifetime.

Another important aspect of energy work, which I want to bring to your attention, is that nearly all cultures train us to suppress emotions and energies and do not allow for the occurrence of certain events or experiences to come to the surface and being expressed until we feel we are capable of dealing with them. —I call that suppression or intentional hiding of your true emotions "noshow;" the opposite of it, the healthy expression of your emotions, which I call "emoshow," is recommended to transform patterns faster.

When we came to the planet, we learned not to speak our truth because no one really wanted to hear the truth. We got used to an enormous amount of suppression and self-denial, which is very different from the stance we will take when we do energy work in form of the Ataana Method with SID. We consciously evoke karmic connections and karmic burdens so-to-speak to allow for their healing. We need to learn how to keep our energy work going once we bring karmic patterns to the surface so that it can start transforming. For instance, if we deal with a past life trauma, it might first appear to be very heavy and challenging, but the Ataana Method and SID are going to lighten the load, so we can start dealing with it, and ultimately be able to heal it.

You might wonder in which manner past life traumas could be brought up again in our current lifetime. It will happen in a way in which we are facing the same traumatic situation as it had been in our past, but with our tuned-in awareness and with energy work, we will be able to offer a different response to it. We are not going to react to it anymore as we did in the past. With the Ataana Method and SID, we will overcome that trigger point for that specific pattern and by overcoming the trigger point we will be able to ultimately transform the pattern.

Maybe it seems as if we were to bring through energy work unnecessary difficulties into our lives. That's not the case. We are conditioned to re-live traumatic experiences over many lifetimes until trauma is successfully mastered, and hence resolved for good. If we were to choose not to engage in energy work, we would merely encounter the same traumatic experiences sooner or later *without* the tools to break the cycle.

Our momentum that needs to persist resides in keeping up the Ataana Method and SID. Keep clearing and keep the momentum. Our daily energy work is like bolstering up a hovercraft that allows us to hover above the ground. We can float above the ground, we can go over water, over oceans and land without touching the ground, we overcome obstacles, yet we are always in a safe space.

By us doing so, we put ourselves in a safe place where transformational issues that are coming up are not working as blockages against us anymore because we can float over them or through them. That's what energy work does for us: even if you face obstacles in front of you, you are like a hovercraft, you are floating through them, or hover over them. You can see them for what they are. Once they don't hold you back any longer as a problem, you can appreciate them for the learning opportunities that they are, and once you appreciate them, they will be transforming even faster.

9. THE KEY TO TRANSFORMATIONAL WORK

The key of transformational work
is keeping the momentum.

I wish to repeat it with all intensity: The key to transformational work is keeping the momentum. —I myself needed about twenty to twenty-five years to build up the momentum of applying daily energy work on myself. There is a part of me that feels like once we feel energetically awesome and great, and we are super-charged, we should just stay like this forever. We are kind of in this place where we become unrealistic in our expectations. It is almost as if we were to decide we are so clean today that we will not need a shower anymore tomorrow or ever again. It's like reveling in our state that feels great to us and deducing, "I should be clean everyday without having to do anything for it." Once you come out of the shower and are clean, and put on cologne or essential oils, you suddenly feel convinced, "I should always be like that."

Reality is there is dust on this planet and all kinds of pollution. If you don't keep clearing yourself, you're going to be dusty. The clearer and cleaner you are, the clearer and cleaner the manner in which you can deal with obstacles. Keeping your energy clear is energy hygiene, and that means doing energy work every day. You start clearing your energy, and the more you clear up, the more you stay clear, and you will start applying it to all other areas of your life as well. Instead of worrying about a situation, find the solution. You can start doing energy work on that situation. For example, if you have bills to pay, you should be doing energy work on these bills to find the ideal solution. You should not be worrying about these bills but merely do energy work on them and allow prosperity energy to enter the situation. You can get a citrine, prosperity stone, from us, or from another spiritual source, and put a citrine on the bills so that they can be energized, and they can be paid off. Do the same with credit cards. Instead of worrying how to pay your bills and credit cards, put them in one stack and do energy work on them until you find a way. Of course, I highly recommend to look also into my Prosperity Healing Mantras if you work on improving your prosperity. As an energy and crystal healer, I often recommend clients to work with my Crystals and Gemstones to facilitate a speedy clearing of issues or to reach specific goals.

You can, by the way, lay the citrine also on your body. I suggest for most of my clients to place a specific gemstone on different areas of their body to workout specific issues or reach goals faster. Here is one of so many examples that I can share with you about adding crystals to the sessions. Two years ago, in Nashville, after several SID and Energy-healing sessions

I instructed Peter, a realtor, to work with a specially-from-me activated citrine for 90 consecutive days to help him overcome stagnation in his business. He was stuck for quite sometime with no deals on the horizon.

He did successfully complete the 90 days as promised. Two days later, the 92nd day after I gave him the stone, he attracted a fairly big deal that put into motion what would become his most successful year so far (overall sales of $68 million dollars that year). I work with many Realtors, who are just jewels of human beings, who improve their performances and approach to life. I observe how they reach the highest levels of self-healing and success with the help of Energy work, SID and Crystal healing.

You can apply the same method to projects you have to accomplish. Write them all down and start doing SID, energy work and crystal healing on each project before you do anything physically about it. You should always do energy work first. By doing so, you bring healing energy to any project or situation, and that means raised consciousness. You will see that the action follows much easier after having applied energy work than if you had to do it all by yourself.

You can do energy work on everything that you are working on or dealing with in any capacity. Fill the project up with energy work first. Similar to what I am doing with this book here. I am doing energy work on it. We are putting energy into this book and that will speed up the process. It will make it more complete. On top of that magnificent reward of completion, you have also charged whatever object, project or situation with magnetic energy. The energy is magnetic enough to attract solutions, which benefits you and everyone else who comes into contact with it. If you want to go deeper and learn the Ataanamethod form of energy work, my online course is available at www.ataanamethodclass.com, or find my certified Ataanamethod teachers close to you.

10. FACILITATING SELF-HEALING

I consider myself an energy healer, and that is what I mean by saying I do energy work: Ultimately, when I—or you—do energy work on others, all we are doing is recharging them so they can attract the right solution to whatever challenge they are facing. Their issue is being energized, so it attracts the right solution. The right solution might be a different attitude, or finding the perfect person or therapist or surgeon or doctor or holistic practitioner or chiropractor, acupuncturist or massage therapist. For the energy knows. The issue in itself knows the right solution, so that's what we are energizing. Energy work is always solution-based healing.

At this point in my life, I am more of a self-activating healer than a healer. In fact, I consider myself a self-healer because I'm supporting my clients in their self-healing process. I'm supporting you to start the self-healing process.

Once you recognize that the person that you are working with starts the self healing process you see his body and system can self heal. Then, you will start to recognize that you are in a self-healing process as well. Self-healing is the key. When you hurt your little finger, your body is not saying, "Why did you hurt yourself? How dumb! Why didn't you use that pair of scissors? Why did you use the carpet-knife?" It doesn't stop the self-healing process. No. When you are bleeding, your system is concerned with one thing and one thing only: how to heal yourself and stop the bleeding. Healing work of this kind yields the least amount of karmic impact for the practitioner.

That's what I'm activating in you. Allowing the self-healing to take place. There is some parts in the system that say, "You don't deserve this healing. You don't deserve to be well. You don't deserve to be prosperous," but the self-healing that I am helping you to funnel will respond to the self-healing request, and activate the self-healing in you. Then you are giving yourself permission to activate the self-healing ability in you. The moment you give yourself permission, the healing process starts taking place.

That's really what my work is about. In the past, I was rather a miracle healer. My approach was, "Let me heal you." Now I am like, "Let me respect you and activate your self-healing so you can heal yourself" because you know best what you need. You know best what you are dealing with, and what the perfect response to your situation is.

I can tell you that you are dealing with this or that, but I can also give you the tools and activate the self-healing in you, and once the self-healing is activated, you can start taking care of yourself. That's why I give you this tool of Sacred Inner Dialogue, so you can start your self-healing.

I am reminding you. By reminding you of your own healing power, it is maybe not the most spectacular healing, like a Christ Angel healing would be where I am moving my arms and levitate in front of you. Activating your self-healing is not spectacular. Healing and wellbeing is basically the expression of harmony and balance in your system.

My task is supporting you to start the self-healing process, and what I am doing with a lot of people is monitoring their self-healing. Then

I say, "This is great. Can you put some energy in this area?" or "What if we concentrate a little bit on this side? What would that look like?" That's really what I am doing. I am helping people with energy work and SID, with the method that I have, to activate their self-healing, which is the ultimate healing. When another system applies their healing on you, your system is not considering this as a fully acknowledged, integrated, and understood experience. It remains unsatisfying and incomplete because someone else did it for you.

Until you change that piece, you have not reached a true breakthrough. That's what is at the base of my healing modality. I throw the ball back to you and I say, "What do you feel needs to happen?" Then, you go to a psychic and they give you insights and tell you, "Do this, this and that." I'm not dissing psychics, I am psychic and clairvoyant myself. They have their place and need to be appreciated in their own right because of the support they give. However, you have to figure it out for yourself, and therefore come to your own conclusions. They tell you, "Do this," and then there's a specific outcome. Ultimately, you still haven't come to your own trust conclusion and made your own decision. You have to be in the driver's seat, not in the passenger seat of your life. You have to drive your vehicle, your life, and move forward by saying, "I listen and follow my own intuition, this decision right now, I am feeling good about and I am moving forward."

Everyone can be weakened at some point and ask for help. In some situations, that's the best thing to do. I totally understand. But my work is self-empowerment. I acknowledge that everyone can realize their full potential and is part of the divine. Everyone has the ability to access their full unlimited power. I help people to get there. That is the key to my work today and to this modality. It might be different with others who want to lay their hands on someone and say, "Everything is going to be fine. You are going to be better." That's okay too, I did that myself for a long time.

However, until you do the essential groundwork and make the essential decision, it is not going to be done for you. Do you and I have miracle and healing powers? Of course, we all have that. For me it is nicer when you step into your power and you ultimately heal yourself because that is when you acknowledge your full potential. My work is more for the awakened person who is aware of their unlimited potential and want to access it. With SID you "Discover your inner voice, your inner truth, your intuition and psychic abilities, which are then going to lead you on your path."

When you come to me, there is a sense of self-activation and of liberation. You truly grow into your power and acknowledge, accept and appreciate your full potential. Could I tell you what to do? Sure I can, but you would not fully integrate the "Why." Mostly I would tell you to do more energy work with my modality to find your own answers.

Once you do something and say, "I'm done with this. I'm going to do that", you know why you are done with something, and you know why you are going to do something else. You are changing your actions to have a different experience, to have a deeper insight: you really "get it." You totally understood that the old route is not getting you anywhere and you are ready to go another route and approach your prosperity, or any aspect you worked on, in a different manner.

Observe through energy work where you have a deficiency in your system, and balance it out energetically, balance with energy work. By balancing any imbalances and deficiencies through the energy work, you are already starting to feel better. As you feel better, you don't feel deficient or have a weird feeling in the stomach, and it is easier to approach the problematic subject. Since you don't feel deficient, you have enough energy to go into a past life, to look at whatever aspect wants to be seen and acknowledged, because you feel it does not take a toll on you. That is why you can now direct your consciousness more effectively to a negative experience of your past without it turning into a traumatic experience all over again.

I will not make you relive a traumatic experience. I am simply taking you there to see and understand it. It is as if I was taking you in a spaceship or time-machine, but you don't have to step outside of it. It doesn't take any fuel either because you are not in a place of deficiency. I provide you with more than enough energy and energy boosts. You are shielded from traumatic effects.

For instance, you can go back in time onto the battlefield and see yourself being butchered, but say, "Woah, that was a tough life" with- out feeling it in a negative way. You're still feeling a warm, fuzzy feeling of having enough energy throughout the session. You are in a nice warm cocoon to feel love and energy, content like a baby in a crib, just breathing. Then we go into these past lives, and I ask you, "Do you think you can address your past-life experience and ask it if it can start the self-healing process?" or, "Why don't you ask the cause of this conflict? Is there anything I can do for you?" or, "Why don't you take a step back and ask the conflict to give you more space, so you can look at this past life?"

I inform you, "We are going in a time capsule and each time there is any form of discomfort, we can immediately shift to a different place. However, don't go before it gets uncomfortable because I can recognize it and protect you from it to happen." If you dare to go there, you will learn, understand and heal.

You are in a safe space. You're not feeling the conflict of that time or the pain of being attacked, so you can release stress and trauma without having to endure anything adverse. We can ask, "Who is fighting you?" Most people recognize in their past life antagonist a person from their close circle of the life they are living now, or someone whom they have encountered sometime earlier in their life, or someone who might be close based on family relations or other social constellations, but with whom they have had a lot of conflict so far or lots of interactions of any kind.

11. CASE STUDIES ON SELF-WORTH AND FAMILY PATTERNS

In the following case studies, we can observe the Sacred Inner Dialogues unfolding and see how SID is neutralizing, dissipating and ultimately transforming any harmful patterns. By addressing the feeling attached to an unhealthy thought pattern, we can also see how the system is being reprogrammed. The conversation with clients does not only focus on the story of who, what, where, and why (although that is how we are able to pinpoint the feeling and unhealthy thought pattern which manifested a challenging episode in the client's life), but we talk directly to the inner subconscious energy. We talk to the inner subconscious energy because these thoughts have grown energetically from the unconscious into mental, emotional, spiritual and physical manifestations. Our conscious mind can grasp these manifestations but the root still resides in the subconscious, which we now address directly. When we address these energies at their root and ask them questions as if talking to another person, these inner thoughts, feelings and deprivation patterns are being addressed, so they feel acknowledged and respond to us. The answers we receive from them are greater clues, and provide us with information on how to solve the root problems of any issues.

This process works across all
patterns, issues and lifetimes.

A. CARRIE: SELF-WORTH AND
FAMILY PATTERNS

Carrie is in her mid-forties and she had felt throughout her entire life a lack of self-worth whenever the suffering of her mother and grandmother are mentioned by her, she falls into a sense of despair that is characterized by a lack of self worth. When she tells her story, the deprivation pattern that affects her can be felt in her heart. I ask her to repeat the following out loud:

"The deprivation pattern that is affecting my family and me, can you hear me?" It answers "Yes." At this point, we acknowledge it.

I ask her where she feels the energy. She says she feels it around her heart. Based on Carrie's story, I know that is exactly where the energy is being felt. It is because she has unmet desires and aspirations, the same feelings her mother and grandmother had, but they had to do something else in life, which felt compromising. Carrie suffers from this same family pattern, however, she has the opportunity to transform it now.

I now ask Carrie to say out loud, "The deprivation pattern that's affecting my family and me, please start the self-healing process now." We have to repeat this out loud a few times, but afterwards a shift in the heart is felt. This brings us deeper into the root issue of addressing her compromised feeling of self-worth. I ask her to say out loud, "My compromised self-worth, can you hear me?" Again, we see if she acknowledges it and receives some sort of response. When she does, I ask her to say out loud, "My compromised feeling of self-worth, please start the transformational process now and raise my self-worth to a higher level."

B. CLAIRE: HEALTH, FAMILY, CAREER AND LOSS

Claire works sixty-five hours a week at a car-dealership financing loans for people. She has multiple sclerosis (MS) and feels she has to continue in her job for a while until she accumulates enough money to make the transition into something more creative, such as realizing her long-standing idea for a book that she wishes to write and publish.

She already believes that everything in existence is energy and it is a matter of figuring out what the energy is that she is working with in order to transform it. She has tried a lot of different things.

She explains her journey, "You graduate at one level and find something else. You still don't feel whole. I don't know if it has been a long dark night of a soul, but it's been about fifteen years of focus and work dedicated to figuring out what is going on with me. I didn't mean for this to turn into a career." In the end she recognizes it is just energy, which is what led her to me. She says, "I feel there are two things that are at play, which are interconnected, but I can't seem to figure out what the energy is. Still, I know, everything is energy and your life experience depends on how you work with it and how you overcome certain energetic blockages and obstacles. I really think that my MS is somehow related to the time when I started healing a long-term eating disorder. I think the energy didn't have anywhere to go and it turned into MS. That's my theory, my gut instinct. I am in therapy and trying to heal what started the eating disorder. I think it's the energy pattern with my mom and only recently, in the last year, I've been working with a therapist that works with archetypal energy, which makes sense."

She continues to say her mom is awesome, yet thinking of her mother triggers her to go into a place that holds a lot of negative energy. It seems to be an archetypal energy, and at the core of the eating disorder resides the wish to die. Claire believes if she can only figure out the pattern, then she can shift it. However, it is her experience that it is also often challenging to figure out your personal issues because you cannot continuously be a witness of your own life when you are in the thick of it.

Claire was also affected by the financial crisis and recession of 2007/08 and was dealing with the death of her brother, who—like her—had suffered from multiple sclerosis for many years. He died from a heart attack. She wants to live a healthier and easier life without scrutinizing every miniscule aspect of it, and sometimes she thinks it is easier to take medication, regardless the side effects, and live as long and as happily as she can. What she is potentially prescribing for herself is a life of numbness through the long-term consumption of significant amounts of medications that would compromise her in various ways. That is particularly of concern given that she has already reached a higher level of consciousness.

I tell Claire that we are going to talk to every emotion, or at least identify every emotion we want to communicate to, as if we would be talking to someone outside of ourselves. She has many emotions and feelings coming up at once and we can begin to address them one by one in this session. I can tell that it is first necessary to clear the passing of her brother and ask her to observe internally, in her mind and energy field, if she receives a response of a yes or no or feels an energy sensation.

I ask her to say out loud, "My grief about my brother's passing, can you hear me?" She feels a sensation like hearing a screaming noise, and states she does not want to deal with it right now. It is too painful. She does not have the energy for it. She says, "I want to deal with the stuff about my mom." She explains that she really thinks that this is where her personal problems correlate. She doesn't know why. Claire thinks it might be because her mother had four children and she didn't have time for everybody, and also because the mother has shown herself to be mentally unstable. She came from a very difficult home as did Claire's dad and her parents tried to contain their own pain over never having received what they needed, both ending up living in their own worlds. Her parents were narcissistic in their own ways, and they just couldn't really see anybody else. Claire concludes, "I think it has to do with not being seen."

Claire cannot understand how a woman such as her mother, who suffers from paranoia and an eating disorder, could have kids. She wonders, "How can an unhealthy person raise healthy children? There's no way, right?" But I want to know what feelings this thought triggers in her. Claire responds, "I feel rage with her. Frustration and rage."

I ask her to say out loud, "The frustration and rage towards my mother, can you hear me?"

Claire repeats this out loud, "The frustration and rage towards my mother, can you hear me?" and then she answers, "Yes, I can hear it."

Then I ask her to say out loud, "The frustration and rage towards my mother please give me more space so I can have healthy thoughts." I ask her to observe her body and see what's going on.

Claire now pictures herself with a bat trying to release the energy. She feels she can control the energy flow by beating it with a bat. This is suppressed anger and rage. I ask her to say out loud, "Any suppressed anger and rage that is still in my system, can you hear me?"

She repeats this and answers, "Definitely. For sure." We begin to see the different layers of frustration, anger, and rage within her. I tell her to let the frustration and rage know it's time for it to start the transformational process and give her more space.

She says out loud, "Frustration and rage, it's time to give me more space and start the transformational process."

She doesn't quite get the words right and has to repeat the sentence three times before she senses her energy is willing to shift into this new space. She feels very exhausted. She acknowledges it on a deeper level by saying, "If most of your energy is going to exhaustion, how can you have energy towards the day, towards what you want? My trauma is constantly competing for my energy."

I ask her to say out loud, "My exhaustion, can you hear me?"

She says it out loud and receives the response, "Yeah, very weary."

I tell her to address her exhaustion, "My exhaustion, please give me more space so I can fully recharge."

She repeats the statement, and then hears, "Sure."

She begins to feel more relaxed and senses her energy levels rising.

Now that she has more energy, we can address deeper issues. I ask her to say out loud, "The dysfunctional energy in my lineage that's also affecting me, can you hear me?" She repeats it. She definitely hears it. She then says, "The dysfunctional energy in my lineage that's also affecting me, please start the self-healing process."

The next steps are more automatic.

"My being tired of living life, can you hear me?"

She repeats it.

"My being tired of living life, please start the transformational process and give me more space." She repeats it and feels a black cloud. I have her repeat the command several times until it feels right. She feels now more life force coming back to her.

"Any hopelessness or helplessness that's still in my system, can you hear me?" She repeats it.

"Any hopelessness or helplessness that's still in my system, please start the transformational process and give me more space." She repeats it three times.

I ask her if she can feel the energy flow on the left side. She lights up. "Yes," she says. Claire feels she has put herself in a tricky situation in life. She says, "Because of my level of exhaustion, I truly sold myself short. You know the stuff that gives you passion and lights you up, you got to have some energy for it. I go to a job that depletes all my energy and depletes my life force. I don't want to be there. It's a tricky thing because you still have to support yourself, and you don't feel secure in the new space (the space where you could potentially be living your passions) to take on your goals and dreams. On a daily basis, I am hurting myself. You see what I mean? It's tricky. How can I get out of that?"

I respond, "Your mother is symbolically speaking a representation of the female supporting energy in the Universe. And your rage towards your mother indicates that you have rage towards your supportive energies, since you did not feel fully supported neither these energies, nor by your mother."

Claire confirms that she has never thought of that. I continue to say, "Since she is the female representation of the caring and nurturing energy, even though she never lived up to that, that's how you feel towards her.

And that's what shaped your feeling of being, or rather not being, supported, for example, by Mother Earth. Mother Earth is also a big mother, the Goddess energy in the Universe. The caring and nurturing energies are often female energies."

Claire acknowledges that when it comes to trust, she doesn't trust that things will ever be okay. "A lot of people turn to God or whomever," she says. "I don't feel a lack of faith, it's rather like I cannot trust… probably because of what you're saying."

"Exactly," I say. "And that's something you can shift. You have to look at it in terms of you getting stuck by your mother. Every time you think about your mother, you get stuck and this prevents you from asking for the bigger picture, from asking for the bigger support from the Universe, because you feel you're not going to get it anyway."

She responds, "I always feel like that. I feel like I don't need anybody or anything. I had to learn to be self-reliant like that. But actually I do need others."

I've seen this pattern with many people. I tell her, "Here's how we can bypass your mother."

I ask her to say out loud, "Caring, mothering and nurturing energies in the Universe, can you hear me?" Claire repeats it and acknowledges a "Yes" response, but she feels no relationship to the source of this response.

I understand she received a faint response, which is positive for her situation. I then ask her to repeat out loud, "Caring, mothering and nurturing energies in the Universe, please become fully present in my everyday life."

"That was amazing," she says, after repeating it three times. "I can physically feel the support. It's almost like you are in a swimming pool and you have a life-raft, and now I can feel the energy expanding." She feels she is no longer part of the living dead, which is how she had felt most days with her life situation—with her mother and the high number of work hours.

I tell her she just reached a place where the picture changed for her fundamentally. Claire had been upset that her mother was standing in the way of her full expansion by not giving her the support she would have needed. Metaphorically speaking, the eating disorder was a manifestation of feeling energetically starved. Claire being the caring, loving mother in her own life is now able to draw from the caring, mothering and nurturing energies of the Universe that are abundantly all around and in her, and she does not focus any longer on her mother, the source of her former disappointments and lack of trust.

Although Claire had a roof over her head and had food on the table, she was at the same time energetically starving because of the dysfunctional use of energy in her family. The energy was not utilized and distributed correctly. Her self-absorbed parents, who had not been able to resolve their own unhealthy patterns and to create a positive way of having their own needs satisfied, basically had taken Claire's life force. Claire gave her life force willingly in the beginning. She didn't work when she was born, so she gave her parents energy in order for them to create a living and feed her. When she left her parent's home years later, thousands of miles away, she took the feelings with her. They still lived inside of her, which means her energy was being sent to her family and into those family patterns.

We now focus on returning all her energy, her life force, back to her.

She is asked to say out loud, "All of my life force that is currently not in my body, can you hear me?"

She receives a response, and then I instruct her to speak after me: "All of my life force that is currently not in my body, please fully return to me and stay with me."

She repeats it. Her energy is jumping for joy. She feels really good right now. I tell her there is still energy, a frequency, a part of her life force that is still not fully accessible to her, or not fully present. It's nice that she's feeling a little bit better, but we are going the full monty, not just being grateful that we are feeling a little bit better. We are not going for existing here, we are going for thriving. Claire feels fascinated because she feels her energy, her thoughts and her vibrantly alive body. It is a completely different frequency that resonates peace and joy. There is nothing causing it from the outside. It is coming from the inside. I tell her that we are going after the trigger that effects the changes from the inside. That's really what we are going after. We are going after that dynamic and that pattern that have caused her pain. It is almost like an implant. When the trigger is activated, it is like the frequency turns into something else. Such trigger reminds me of a mega-large faucet; when you turn it on it drains your life force very fast.

I tell her there's one more thing of which I want to make her aware:

"Remember the moment we were talking about the faucet installation, and once it is open, it drains your life force really fast? That was something that was installed in you when you were younger. You were lying there in a crib and basically giving all your life force to your parents who were taking care of you. They needed life force. They needed energy because they didn't feel they could go on all the time either." Claire says, "That's what I've come to believe."

I continue to explain, "Your parents were in a place where they could barely make ends meet, and they said, 'Oh my goodness, how are we going to take care of all these children? How are we going to make this all happen?'" They got totally overwhelmed. It's understandable. What they did happened because they didn't know any better. They basically installed in every child an energy faucet."

This is a normal process. Don't misunderstand me: They are not evil or anything. Children can't live by themselves, so they employ the mother and father to work for them and in exchange send their parents life force. What's unfolding is a subconscious contract, where the parents are installing energy faucets to take life force.

That faucet connects through a hose to the parents. Once the faucet is opened, the life force of a child is being sent to them. For the child, it doesn't really matter because there is so much energy, like crazy energy, a whole lot. The child feels like, " That doesn't matter. I have 100% energy, and 25% down leaves me still 75% with what is like a 100% percent of a normal human beings life force. I have so much."

What happens when you're growing up is that the parents are not following through with their part of the contract, namely to remove these installations, these faucets. Although they are not working for the children anymore, they are still taking the life force from every child. Now the child is thirty years old and needs to make a living for him- or herself but cannot do it because a lot of the life force is getting zapped by the parents. That is the installation that's still active in Claire's system. I tell her, "I think you are angry at your mother because the installation is still active. So today we are going to remove that installation and that will take care of a whole lot of that anger you feel toward her, and it will regulate the energy imbalance between the two of you."

I ask her to repeat out loud, "Any faucets that are still in my system that my parents installed in me, can you hear me?"

Claire has to say it three times before it comes out complete. She feels a little energy.

I observe and ask her, "It's in your right hand and in your right shoulder. Do you feel that?"

She does. Her mind is somewhat racing because she is now thinking back to her early twenties when she needed guidance but had to give her mother guidance instead. I tell her to say out loud, "Any faucets that are still in my system that my parents installed in me, it is time to be transformed and to be completely released."

She begins to lose focus and I remind her to keep this string alive because it's like we are performing etheric surgery right now. We have to keep this clear, sanitized and don't want anything else in there.

"Let's get your full focus here, Claire. Once we remove these faucets I want you to fill the empty space with pink magenta light. This pink magenta light is like a ceramic filling that you put in your teeth. It is gummy and then it hardens like ceramic so it actually closes that opening, so nothing else goes in there." She gets through it and more space becomes available within her. I ask her to fill that opening with the pink magenta light.

"Now you're going to see how much easier you are going to deal with your mother because she's not going to zap your energy right away. You are not feeling a deficiency immediately and you will not have any reason to get angry at her anymore."

Claire says, "That's so crazy because she has been like my kryptonite. I've been running from my mother, and I don't want to run from her. I want to spend time with her."

I say, "With this pattern in place, you could be two thousand miles away and it would still be draining you. Now you can be standing next to her and she won't drain you. It is going to be a whole new experience." Claire is fascinated by the energetics and my attunement to what's going on with her.

My attention with Claire has been purely on the energetics because that is where everything else comes from. My attention is always purely on the energetics because I know once you shift your energetic frequency a little bit, it makes a difference in the outer manifestation and in how you feel and what you experience.

C. LINA: FAILURE, MOTHER AND LINEAGE PATTERNS

For the following case study that includes work on patterns from one's lineage, I will share with you the dialogue between my client Lina and myself.

Lina: I intend to work on the pattern of not expecting more as to avoid disappointment. I still feel excitement, but then it is easily squashed even before disappointment happens almost as in an effort to brace myself: so that when disappointment happens, it's anticipated already. So I don't feel disappointment. It's a form of self-protection.

A: We know that pattern; we know you saw this pattern from your mother.

L: Yes. She was getting incredibly excited about everything. As a child, I was watching her so often in high hopes for something, and when it did not come through, I saw her disappointment, so I needed a place to protect myself from that.

A: Your mother was already expecting results. She expected them as a certain outcome of a given situation, and when the situation didn't yield that outcome, she was more than frustrated.

L: It was incredible disappointment that she felt.

A: This was a most profound disappointment.

L: Her expectations were never met.

A: Her expectations were never met, and as we know, she was dealing at the time also with addiction. She masked the extreme highs and lows experienced through her addiction as her not getting what she wanted after she had been anticipating it with such excitement and the "understandable" disappointment. She used this strategy to distract from her addiction. You were watching her behavior and saw that most of the time, your mother did not get what she wanted, and it caused profound low points in her life. By you seeing that, you subconsciously decided to protect yourself from the same drama by only not staying in the middle of life's joys and satisfactions, but below the middle. So you have the monotone experience of not creating too big of an expectation ever for yourself, so you will never experience too big of a disappointment.

A healthy anticipation would be to forcefully declare, "I want this. Regardless of the outcome, I will put my all into it. I'm still going for it." And by going for it with all of your desire, willpower and persistence, you'd be creating the outcome that you desire!

L: But my mother went for it and didn't get it, and that's what I had been seeing.

A: But your mother didn't go for it 100%, otherwise she would have gotten it. She went pretty far but if she had given 100% to it, it would have manifested. She went probably 99% and most likely she gave up, or for whatever other reason, it didn't come through. If something does not come through, it's not because people do everything they can do, they probably fall short in some way or form. There can be some things you try and try and it just doesn't work. That's almost like you put all of your energy into it, and then you pray, and you are fully open and surrender to what happens. Then you're not in a state of any disappointment. You simply say, "I know. I did my best. If it didn't happen, it didn't happen."

In contrast to that, you would only build up an unrealistic expectation whenever you decide to go out of the blue for a certain outcome, and you wish for it, and then you put a lot of energy into it, and you expect for it to come through with that exact amount of energy. In that case, you don't really show persistence. Follow up, and follow up again, and when it didn't happen at the first attempt, follow up, and follow up again until it happens. Utilize the resistance as strengthening training like resistance workout until you get stronger, you are not stopping the training just because you could bench a certain weight, goal or reps, or ran a certain distance, often we are going even further and why not if we love what we do?

That's what you have to understand. As a child you integrated this unhealthy pattern when you saw your mother in vain trying to get something, whatever it was.

L: That's true. I saw that happening with everything my mother ever wanted. Relationships. Money. Everything.

A: If you go into all of these aspects, and you really stay focused on the subject, and put yourself out there all the time with the firm purpose to get what you want, and you make a commitment and you persist in your belief and efforts, then it's going to happen. But you didn't see it coming through in the past, and your mother made you believe she gave it her all. That's the misunderstanding. "Hey I'm trying the best I can do," is what she would have said, but actually she didn't. Because if she would have left everything else behind that could have been a hindrance on her path of being the best person she could be in order to manifest what she wished for, she would have most likely achieved it. That means her addiction was obviously in the way.

The same holds true for other character flaws. They are often in the way when we fail even though we think we nearly gave our all. If you approach any internal flaws first and then your goals, you will start attracting it, or transforming in such way that what you desire comes into your life. That's when one can truly say, "I tried everything I could." Only then you can say, "I understand. I put my whole being into it."

If you didn't put your whole being into it and then it didn't happen but you expected it to happen and you adopt this as your outlook, then you created for yourself a formula for setting yourself up for failure over and over again, if that makes sense. That's the pattern you're dealing with. You're dealing with, "I am not putting my whole being into it because I had not seen her put her whole being into it." You just adapted to the pattern because that pattern was a reality for you when you watched your mother as a child. Now you're thinking, "Well, I really kind of want to do everything to achieve my goal, but how to put my whole being into it? Who showed me ever how to put my whole being into it? I was only being shown to do a lot towards a goal, and then say, "This is everything I have" and fail.

I believe that's the pattern that's running. No one wants to hear, "I'm not doing enough." It's not really about that. It's about the fact that there is a certain measure of effort that you invest in establishing the ultimately unsatisfying reality for you that says, "I did everything because I did just as much as my mother."

You say, "Hey, my mother tried this up to this point, and then she was disappointed because it didn't happen." It's like learning an instrument and you say, "I'm giving myself six months. By then I want to play this instrument like the best violinist, or guitar player." If it doesn't happen after six months, then it's a disappointment. And then you throw the instrument away or break it.

Why do I dwell on this so much, Lina? It's a really good pattern for us to understand crucial aspects of ourselves, and of how we can make changes in our lives.

If you see the full spectrum of such ingrained pattern in somebody's life, it's easier for you to approach it. If you wouldn't talk about this, Lina, you would just let go of the pattern of "doing everything you can, but results still don't come through." That's not the reality. The reality is that your mother didn't try everything she could have done, and then she failed. That's the reason why she failed. The pattern is not right.

L: It's a self-imposed ceiling.

A: It gives you a marker that says, "Look. When she tried to brainwash you and said, "I did everything I could, but see that it didn't happen"—i.e. in situations when your mother felt unjustly neglected by God and the Universe, it was actually never the case that she was neglected at all. Lina, that's the pattern you're transforming because you are now with Sacred Inner Dialogue going into a system where you say, "I do it and I'm going to give it my best." Once you give it your best, it's going to happen. You can look to about any self-help book, or to about any religion: If you try and you give it your best, most likely it's going to happen.

What this means is that perseverance is needed. Getting it done with just one push, that's magic. Reality is that you are like an apprentice for the Universe and the Creator, and you keep on learning and integrating and growing in this process of facing challenges with perseverance and ultimately with success. That's your journey that is unfolding. A lot of people don't want to be on this journey. They say, "either give me what is mine or I want to get out of here." However, that's like a giving up, a failure program. It's like putting stipulations on the Universe. The Universe says, "Sure. If that's what you want and you want that frame, let's do it. But it's going to unfold in its own reality!" Any time limitation you're putting on the Universe, is just a way of limiting yourself. If you approach anything with, "I love this. I can do this for the rest of my life. It doesn't take any effort. I could do this for the next one hundred years. It doesn't matter if my desired outcome comes about today or in twenty years from now, or even whether it happens at all." Most likely the Universe is going to manifest for you what you desire with more ease than you could have ever imagined.

Even when people know it, they still don't do it.

L: It's counterintuitive to act this way when you want something.

A: If you go about it in 3-D reality. A big part of this is approaching it in a way in which you can love it. In this reality, it's counterintuitive to say I love giving my all to something because most people are working in a job, or on projects that they don't love. So loving something is not even an option because they hate what they do. Most of the people fall into this category. Very few people love what they do and they are successful for some reason. A lot of people would rather hate what they do and maintaining that paradigm instead of going into something they really love to do. Ideally, the first thing we want to establish is that whatever we want to do, we should be connecting to the energy of love for doing it, and that connection has to be (re-) established.

Enough of, "If I get this, then I love life. If I don't get it, I hate life." That's a blackmail program. When you say to life, "It doesn't matter. I don't care if I get it or not. God, whatever you want is ok with me." Once you accept that, you can start effectively working on goals and attract them, or not. It doesn't really matter to the Universe. Let me rephrase it. It does matter to the Universe in the sense that the Universe is going to listen to you and provide you with the experiences for which you seem to ask: You're putting out there something that you don't love, so the Universe thinks what you don't love is what you want more of. The Universe wants to serve you so it brings you more of it. —If you start loving what you're doing, the Universe wants to give you more of that because obviously that's what you're loving. Whatever we represent in the Universe or send out to the Universe as our reality on a 24-hour basis, or 7-day basis, that's what the Universe thinks is what we want. Why would we otherwise choose it, since we can just as easily choose anything else?

That's the idea of us focusing on what we love to do. Once we established our focus on what we love to do, that's when we're going to attract more of that what we love.

Let's now transform this pattern.

C1 . LINA DIVES DEEPER TO TRANSFORM THESE PATTERNS

We are now ready to transform this pattern, and I ask Lina to speak the following words to begin a SID:

L: My belief system *that I can't get excited about what I want* because otherwise I am met with disappointment, can you hear me?

A: Let my belief system *that I can't get excited about what I want* now know that it is time to be transformed and replaced with a healthier belief system.

L: My belief system *that I can't get excited about what I want*, it is time now for you to be transformed and to be replaced with a healthier belief system.

A: This new healthier belief system is, "I give myself permission to be excited about opportunities and I give myself permission to have everything that I desire."

L: This new healthier belief system is, "I give myself permission to be excited about opportunities and I give myself permission to have everything that I desire."

A: I can achieve and accomplish everything.

L: I can achieve and accomplish everything.

A: I now invite the energy of excitement into my life.

L: I now invite the energy of excitement into my life.

A: The installation that protects me from disappointment can you hear me?

LI: The installation that protects me from disappointment can you hear me?

L: Yeah.

A: Please start the transformational process now.

L: Please start the transformational process now.

A: Me not having to feel devastated from disappointment anymore, can you hear me?

L: Me not having to feel devastated from disappointment anymore, can you hear me?

L: Yeah.

A: Please become fully present now.

L: Please become fully present now.

A: MY excitement about life, can you hear me?

L: MY excitement about life, can you hear me?

L: Yeah.

A: Please replace any form of disappointment in my system.

L: Please replace any form of disappointment in my system.

A: Any of my mother's programs that are not healthy for me and are still active, can you hear me?

L: Any of my mother's programs that are not healthy for me and are still active, can you hear me?

L: Yeah.

A: Please start the transformational process.

L: Please start the transformational process.

L: I knew that one was going to come up in this one. I was thinking about that on the way over here. I think it's a lineage thing. It's not just my mom.

A: Any programming in my lineage that held us back from living our full potential, can you hear me?

L: Any programming in our lineage that held us back from living our full potential, can you hear me?

A: Ask it to start the transformational process now and to be completely released.

L: I ask you to start the transformational process now and to be completely released.

A: Me letting go of my mother's measure of effort, can you hear me?

L: Me letting go of my mother's measure of effort, can you hear me?

A: Please start the transformational process and be replaced with a healthy measure.

L: Please start the transformational process and be replaced with a healthy measure.

A: The healthy measure is, "I give it my all. I am receiving it all."

L: The healthy measure is, "I give it my all. I am receiving it all."

A: The healthy measure is I'm giving it my all and I reach my goal.

L: There's a blockage because my mom worked so hard that I said I'm never going to do that. There's a blockage between what I know I can do and what I actually do…

A: We're going to refine that a little bit more. It's not implying getting to the point of exhaustion when you're giving it your all. When you're giving it you're all, you're planning it, you're all. You're preparing all. The work part is just 25% of it. Another 25% is timing, planning, etc.

L: Because giving it my all, to me, is seeing her being wiped out.

A: No, that's not what this is about. We have to refine this in words.

A: My new program is now, "I'm planning accordingly to reach my goal."

L: My new plan? What is it? Somehow the word healthy has to be in there… It's like healthy planning or healthy organization….

A: My new healthy program is, "I plan according to my resources to reach my goal."

L: My new healthy program is, "I plan according to my resources to reach my goal."

D. GLORIA: LINEAGE TRAUMA OF LOSING PROPERTY AND WEALTH

As the following case study illustrates even more so than Lina's, we need to go back into a person's lineage for the transformation of any patterns that have been passed on from generation to generation. In this case, the grandfather of my client Gloria had his properties, homes, land and wealth taken away from him by the Cuban government prior to Castro becoming the country's leader. There are a thousand stories in the family that have been emerged based on this programming: Gloria believes she cannot have what she wants and it doesn't matter what she has, it can be taken away from her. This makes her very careful in creating anything because anything being created is being taken away.

Her system is very careful in accumulating wealth in any form, whether it is richness in relationships, health, wealth or in anything. She appears to be tiptoeing around the mark of the beginning stages of even being on the start line of creating wealth. This is what we have to transform and the reason why we go into the pattern that created this belief system. This belief system was formed after a corresponding reality had been experienced. In Gloria's case, her belief system is based on her grandfather having something that was taken away after the government changed. Her family had to come to another country where her dad wasn't really accepted. He had to work hard and did not receive the promotions he should have gotten. Even in instances when her dad was successful and got everything that he needed, he still somewhere had this program running where he didn't trust society. He didn't trust society because everything he owned was taken away from his family before, so it's really hard for him to trust people now.

This programming had been passed on to Gloria. Without trusting people, she can't successfully engage in teamwork. She creates animosity. Whenever she doesn't trust what's happening around her, she introduces mistrust. There is enough of a challenge to make things run smoothly when you trust everyone and everything around you. Once she trusts she can let go of the mistrust that creates an enormous energy waste. She doesn't have to constantly check, "Is this going fine?" and she can put her energy into doing what she needs to be doing. That's something that's very important for Gloria, or truly for anyone, because it sets into motion to be as successful as she can be. In order to overcome what is happening in her life now, it is required to go back into the lineage to clear the dysfunctional energy that has been present for generations and has been so far shaping Gloria's experience.

I ask Gloria to say out loud, "My belief system that I'm not fully supported by God and the Universe, can you hear me?"

She gets a response and says, "Yes."

We inform this belief system that it is time for it to be transformed and replaced with a healthier belief system by her saying: "My belief system that I'm not fully supported by God and the Universe, it is time for you to be transformed and replaced with a new healthier belief system."

We both come to the conclusion that the new healthier belief system would be "I am fully supporting God and the Universe, and I am fully supported by God and the Universe at all times."

Then we say: "My new belief system, with which I replace my old one, is "I am fully supporting God and the Universe, and I am fully supported by God and the Universe at all times."

Next I ask Gloria to repeat out loud "I am fully supporting God and the Universe, and I am fully supported by God and the Universe at all times" and to repeat this affirmation fifty times a day to create this new reality. Once it becomes her reality we can start going deeper.

12. STRUCTURES, BLUEPRINTS AND FRAMEWORKS

No one really has ever started talking to themselves and acknowledged themselves as unlimited systems. We don't even discern that there are aspects in ourselves like patterns, belief systems, and structures. Sacred Inner Dialogues help to make these structures visible and to show us the blueprints of our lives. The word blueprint is very significant here because everything that we are experiencing in our lives is part of our blueprints. There are systems and programs in place that determine our life experience, and that's why I make frequent comparisons to a computer program. Blueprints program us; like a master printing plate of a banknote that turns blank paper into money, they turn our daily energy into certain experiences. They make us experience certain situations. The more we can identify our internal blueprints, the more we can identify why we are experiencing certain situations. The first step is not just knowing that there is something wrong with us, it's more about being investigative and wanting to know what our specific blueprint looks like. That's the prerequisite to even go into a Sacred Inner Dialogue.

Sacred Inner Dialogues are self-revelatory.
SID is not the right tool for people who
don't want to look at themselves.

People who don't want to look at themselves, don't want to go deeper. They will refuse to go deeper no matter from which angle we approach the issue, no matter what their particular hold up about going deeper or their belief system is.

Before you build a skyscraper, you build a metal ossature with poles and struts, so that they can support the future building, as well as a scaffold around it. Looking at the site, you see a crane up there. You see an emerging structure. There is a scaffold so that people can go up and put the building blocks on top of each other. The scaffold itself is a structure. You first raise a scaffold, and then you start building the core structure.

You can compare this building process with the way in which people create, consciously and unconsciously, the structures, blueprints and frameworks of their lives. People have scaffolds that help them to put up the main frame of their lives. Before there is anything solid being made, it's scaffolds all over the place, until it becomes a recognizable structure as the main structure is being created over a period of time. Whatever the pattern or belief system is, it becomes now a reality. It becomes ingrained, like you're walking a path often and all of a sudden, that path—or pattern, for this matter, becomes more distinct and larger as more people keep walking on it. We have these pathways and scaffolds all over the place internally. Some of them are in place to create a stronger skyscraper, but either way, the framework is something that we have in place for everything that we experience in life. We have a framework that is built up internally from different aspects of qualities of life that we consider important or part of our life. For example, good habits, bad habits, perseverance, procrastination, whatever it is, there's always a framework for it.

See it as a house. The house is your life. Your life is made up of different bricks that contain different qualities of energies that we're creating everyday over long periods of time. These energies might be earning money, going to work, making good decisions, etc. Our life is being built up by these qualities. That is our framework for our life. We can trace it back to our framework how our lives play out. SID helps to make that framework visible. Once you understand the blueprint, then the framework, then the structure, you can imagine that you have now all the components to create a new building, to un-create an existing building, or to add another structure on to it. You have all the consciousness required to make any of these things happen. But first you have to understand the blueprint. You have to understand the framework. You have to understand what this building is made up of. Is there asbestos in it? Is it masonry? Is it steel? What it is made up of? SID helps you to answer these questions.

This is very important to understand. The first and foremost importance of SID is understanding what the blueprint or framework of the structure of your life is. What is our life made up of? What is that person's life made up of? Then you see patterns with the father, with the mother, with family, with God, and patterns with the Universe such as no belief in a higher power. Whatever the belief system, no belief system is still a belief system. Belief systems are put into place so life becomes easier. It's like habits. You don't think about habits you're just doing it.

Habits don't know whether they're good or bad, they're just being put into place.

There is no judgment of that habit prior to you going into the identification of the framework with the help of Sacred Inner Dialogue. That's why SID is very important because it makes visible to us what the internal structure is. Then we can look at the outside: what experiences are going on in the outside world? Now we can translate these experiences back to our blueprint. We can also decide to change the blueprint, and then something in the outside world is going to change, too. Once you understand that, you understand why this is so important. The more you know about your internal structure, the more you understand why it's being put into place, and the more consciousness you have about this, the more you can create the perfect life that you desire. That requires internal communication and most of the people don't even think about talking to themselves and identifying their blueprint because most of them don't even know that they have a blueprint.

This is something for everyone. All of a sudden we recognize that we have the infinity of the Multiverse in ourselves and through our channels from our DNA, from the configuration of the patterns that we created, life energy flows and creates experiences that we have in life. When these building blocks are played in a different way, we have different experiences. It's like having a xylophone: each xylophone stick has a distinct sound like A, B, C, D, E, F, G and we can play them in various combinations

In whatever way you play them, determines the difference in their harmonics, and the type of music experience we are having. Now you understand the principle of how life force is flowing through us. Observing and listening to ourselves, we can also detect how high, strong, or low our self-love is, which makes a big difference in how we experience our lives. If we love our self to the highest degree possible, is there then another higher degree of how we could love ourselves? I'm not posing this question in an egotistical way, but is the frequency maybe so low that it is almost self-hate? This has to be identified. Everyone has self-love, but the question is how high or low is our self-love? Is it at zero, minus ten or plus eight? We can observe that and once we identify the answer to this question, we can start adjusting it. But by us not knowing what is in there, there is no way we could be attentively listening to ourselves and make adjustments to create different, better and healthier experiences. We haven't even taken claim of our internal processes. Most of the people don't want to look into themselves because they are afraid of what they are going to see. For years and years people have suppressed their emotions and energies.

Generally, people were taught not to show emotions and when emotions come up, the first thing they are conditioned to do is to suppress them. Our work here as healer and self-healer is to allow ourselves to understand the power of emotions, the power of the internal world, the power of the internal structure, of the mind, the spirit and the physical body. Our work is to make all internal structures visible. This means structures on all levels: mental, physical, emotional, spiritual and astral.

This means that all levels are working independently within their respective environments and then they also work unified, aligned with each other. When they are in alignment, they create beautiful experiences that allow us to flourish in life. If they are not in alignment, our experiences will reflect that lack of harmony. Even when we mean well, it will then be rather like a whisper in the telephone game: you say one thing and something totally different comes out.

SID helps us to create an internal alignment of our mental, physical, emotional, spiritual and astral levels because we are making all of these systems, frameworks and scaffolds visible so that it is easy to arrange or rearrange them. Once they are visible, we acknowledge them. We don't even think about change yet, let's just acknowledge them first. Occupy yourself entirely with merely acknowledging them. Be fully present with the energy that comes to fore when you apply SID. Ask: By which experiences am I affected right now? —I might be affected by procrastination, by exhaustion, by feeling tired, by feeling I'm not qualified enough, not adequate enough, not confident enough, not strong enough, or not beautiful enough. All these perceived deficiencies have to be acknowledged if they come up. If you do this, it is not going to be like in the past when you might not have wanted to look at something and you were thinking, "I don't want to look at this because nothing happens when I did this before." This time it is different. Acknowledge everything but instead of feeling disempowered by what you see, you rather recognize that these are structures and frameworks that were put into place. They were put in place by ourselves or by somebody else, and they create a certain outcome such as, for instance, not getting what we want. Now once we recognized this, we can ask these qualities to give us more space, or we can go deeper and ask what it is that we can do for these qualities and ask them to start the transformational process so we can truly experience a healing or that we can be living a healthier life.

That has to be done with an unwavering desire of investigating what is happening inside ourselves. Our attitude has to be one of not getting tired of looking into ourselves, not being fed up with what's inside, not being overwhelmed with what's inside, not feeling tired or being exhausted just by looking into ourselves, but rather feeling excited about it: The more we recognize our unlimitedness, the more we see that these structures had been put in place, for some reason, to limit and teach ourselves.

The more we understand that we set out to transform limitation, the more excited we get. We truly live an unlimited life. Now we can open ourselves up to live an expanded, rich, exciting life. SID means we're at the pulse of time: we recognize which part of us is creating what in every given moment. We recognize what we are feeling in the moment. We get more aligned in experiencing truly what we are doing at that moment in real time. We recognize, "I'm feeling limited." —That marks the turning point! Now I can ask: Why do I feel limited?

I can make adjustments: "Limitation, can you hear me?" Once it answers with "Yes," I continue the dialogue: "My limitation, please give me more space." We actually observe ourselves and use SID as a gauge: Where am I doing what out of habit, because of imprinting through my parents, my grandparents, my lineage, or where do I feel I have to limit myself? Then, as I stay focused on my transformation, I can go into the experience of my unlimitedness, into my expansion, into contact with my unlimited Source. Clear observation combined with Sacred Inner Dialogues can make this happen for us. We will recognize that we are all channels of the infinite and we are channeling our infinite selves with millions and billions of qualities, all of which we can draw upon in order to put them into building blocks and frameworks for our lives.

With SID, we can also channel our loved ones who have passed over. We can support them on their transformational path, as well as ask them to support us in our lives or dissolve any unresolved issues related to them.

13. SID CHECKUP AND IMPROVEMENT PROTOCOL

This next section contains enriched protocols for SID: We are going to look at a standard session, and I will show you what needs to be considered in that situation as long as nothing else is coming up and asks for our attention. If nothing else comes forth, you will start a session by following this outline.

*SID is an overall wellness, assessment
and improvement tool.*

It considers all aspects of a person, including our energetic wellbeing. Keep in mind that not every person will be immediately ready to dive deep into her unconscious and explore all facets of her energetic makeup. SID is a wellness improvement procedure that allows for overall consideration of whatever is going on in a person's life. For example, some people who are not (yet) willing to go as deep as might be needed to explore the root causes for any unfavorable life experiences, but they can still receive a very good clearing or procedure with this protocol and feel something really shifted during their session. They might not have had the depth to go there but they felt, "Wow, something shifted." That's something we have to consider. This process can take place either in person or over the phone. Each approach is slightly different. The distance approach is going to be a little different than the in person session, yet both follow the same general outline.

I want to make it visible so that it can be truly a procedure that allows you, as a practitioner, to support the healing process of a client in a structured and meaningful manner. The first step would be the improvement of general life force intake. That marks already an increase in the energy flow of the client. It can be a procedure that ensures that all chakras are in harmony. That all the chakras are balanced and that the client gets enough energy. It includes a clearing of dense energies. Let me go a step further and show you how it is done for your clients as well as for yourself.

MODULE 1: CALLING BACK YOUR LIFE FORCE

Note:

You or your clients need to feel the desire to live life fully. If you are working with a very depressed person who does not want to live, then this procedure would not be a good approach since that person would, presumably, not want to have all his life force back to fully embrace life. The underlying conflict between the protocol and the true desire of the client would turn the session ineffective. (Energy work always respects the will of everyone involved.)

Get a statement from yourself or the other person that you work with that amounts to "I want to fully live my life."

The most important part here is that the person wants to live. A lot of people have in their life experiences where they didn't want to live for some reason. Nearly everyone has this experience more or less prominently in their life stream: there is a moment when they didn't want to live, or couldn't handle what presented itself in their lives, so that they didn't want to live any longer. This can occur subconsciously, without thinking about this, or a person might be almost at the verge of giving up. It could even be something that they were not directly involved in but their parents, or someone they grew up with, had it in their systems and they picked it up too. In that case, there are a few steps that need to be done before any session can really start. These steps are as follows:

"I ask all of my life force that's currently not in my body if it can hear me."

"All of my life force that's currently not in my body, can you hear me?" Once a positive response is received, we continue: "All of my life force that's currently not in my body, please fully return into my body and into my life now."

If clients are only 20 percent in their body, they are not even going to feel a session because they are not even here. The most important thing you can do is to get your clients firmly back into their bodies, into their lives, and make that improved state a new commitment for them now. For everyone who reads my book now, in this moment, say, "I now commit all of my life force to this, my body and my life."

Commit to this statement and now all your life force can return.

Wanting to live your life and calling all your power back is the starting point for all further energy work that will then allow you to go deeper. If your clients are ready to go deeper after this, then you probably have to work with the root chakra because many people are not fully grounded. (Anyone whose life force has been fragmented lacks in being fully grounded in this life.) Sooner or later, if that's the case, you as a practitioner want to work on your own and their root and crown chakras because some of their energy went out and some other energy occupied their chakras. The same holds true for other chakras: your clients did not want to be fully on the planet, and as a result, they have usually something going on with their lower backs or their legs or with other chakras.

We can utilize it for us and our clients to move forward and start the healing process. If your clients are not fully there, then they can't experience the full healing. That's why a lot of people are numb, take a lot of medication, or are "checked out" in general. Look around you. A lot of people are checked out. This procedure is designed to bring people back into their lives and bodies, and then, we can really analyze which part of their chakras is opposing the full energy of being here in this life, on this planet. Is it the heart, the solar plexus chakra, is it the throat chakra, the root chakra? Might it be because of sexual abuse that this person is checked out? Or is it because of another form of verbal, mental, emotional or spiritual abuse? Did this situation first emerge in this life, or is it rooted in a past life? Did your clients not want to live, did it get too hard for them and did they just not want to be on the planet anymore? Part of their energy is checked out. That means part of their system didn't get enough life force to be maintained. We want them to come back into their lives, so we can most effectively work and support them. That's the first and most important step.

If all of our life force would be fully in our bodies, we'd all be levitating and doing the wildest things because we are unlimited energies. We all would be fully tuned into our lives and not tuned out. We want every part of our life force that's not available to us right now to return to us. The more life force we have in our bodies, the more magnetic we are to attract whatever we need and desire. The more magnetic we are, the less we have to use effort to create and attract anything in our lives. The more we dwell in the past or in the future, the more we are not in the present. This is why it is so important to call all of our power back to us. It needs to be the first thing to remember that we are powerful beings. *I call all of my power back to me. I am whole and complete.*— This now all becoming part of our makeup through the conscious use of Sacred Inner Dialogue. Your clients, you yourself, are calling all of your life force that is currently not in the body back to yourself. When we are calling it back, what is happening? Our root chakra has enough energy. Our second chakra has enough energy. We feel energized. We don't feel like we are onlookers in our own lives, but we are in full command of our lives. Once we are on the commander bridge of our lives, we can start changing directions. That's when we are back in charge of our Space ship. That's why this first step is so important.

Start with yourself: "I call all of my life force that's currently not in my body back to myself and into my life." Then ask the person you're working with to speak: "I call all of my life force that's currently not in my body, can you hear me?" Once your client receives a positive response, ask her to speak, "I call all of my life force that's currently not in my body back into my body and into my life."

Note:

In the following, you will encounter additional fourteen modules that allow you to apply Sacred Inner Dialogue virtually to all areas of our system and experience. I recommend you to work through these modules step by step to see results manifest in your life. A pace that yields for most people the most beneficial outcome—without risking of getting overwhelmed by the process—is working on each module for one week before moving to the next module, start reading through it and then apply it.

MODULE 2: RECHARGING YOUR CHAKRAS

This is an essential, yet very simple step. Follow this protocol to work on yourself, as well as with others:

"All of my chakras, can you hear me?"

"YES"

"All of my chakras, please spin in the highest frequency possible."

MODULE 3: GROUNDING

Look also up MULADHARA — I HAVE in MODULE 15.

The root chakra represents our connection to our mother (Mother Earth).

"Anything interfering with my grounding, can you hear me?"

"YES"

"Anything interfering with my grounding, please start the transformational process.

"My compromised grounding, can you hear me?"

"YES"

"My compromised grounding, please start the transformational and healing process now."

(Why is this necessary? —Because your state of being grounded in this life and in this world is compromised. As a practitioner, I want your compromised grounding to start the self-healing process.)

"My fully intact grounding, can you hear me?"

"YES"

"My fully intact grounding, please become fully present and fully activated now."

"Me being fully grounded and connected with Mother Earth, can you hear me?"

"YES"

"Me being fully grounded and connected with Mother Earth, please become fully present now."

MODULE 4: CROWN CHAKRA

Look also up SAHASRARA — I KNOW in MODULE 15.

The crown chakra represents our connection to our Creator, to the Father Source.

"Anything that's compromising my crown chakra, can you hear me?"

As a next step, we ask anything that's compromising the crown chakra to give us more space: "Anything that's compromising my crown chakra, please give me more space."

Once it gives us more space, we can ask it to start the transformational process:

"Anything compromising my crown chakra, please give me more space and start the transformational process."

EXCURSUS: SPACE AND MULTIDIMENSIONALITY, EXPANSION AND USE OF LIFE FORCE

Whenever the situation gets too sticky, or too heavy, or too tough, the intention is: "Please give me more space." That phrase is sufficient to gently ask and to receive just enough space for our next move, whatever it might be.

Why would we desire more space? So that we can unfold into that space. The tiniest bit of space is better than nothing; it gives us more space for our energy.

The more of our energy we have in our energy field, the more magnetic we are, and the more consciousness we attract. A tiny amount of space can be an infinite space in the reality of Multidimensionality since everything is fractaling out up to infinity.

That has to be understood. Everything is a fractal. With every little space I get, I gain infinite space that gives me new freedom for action. A little bit of space is all the space in the world. One space is connected to all space. *One Allness or Aloneness is connected to all Oneness.* (Read this last sentence carefully!) So if we get a little bit of space, we can go into the unlimited space of all space.

Multidimensionality is built like this: It consists of fractals, infinitely complex and never-ending patterns into infinity that are self-similar across different spaces. Whatever I am able to do to change a pattern in one space, even if it might be a small space, affects the patterns in all spaces. Multidimensionality is an infinitely complex, dynamic system that allows us far greater freedom of action, a far greater power of healing, and more agency in creating of our best lives possible than most of us dare to imagine. Everything in a multidimensional universe, or rather multi-verse, is already expanded. Everything turns into expansion. Everything is expansion and everything is unlimited.

Acting in multidimensionality means connecting the frequency of limited space with the frequency of infinite space. This is a process that follows exact laws. You could compare it to quantum physics or string theory. I am accessing reality holographically. What I'm doing at this moment is merely allowing it to become visible. I allow for space, which is already there, to become visible. I am shining a light on the space that is already there, a space that merely was not visible. That space becomes enlightened, and its truly unlimited qualities come forth. That's Enlightenment and expansion.

Ultimately, expansion means not making a space bigger, but making your consciousness bigger, i.e. you expand in your consciousness. You are expanding your awareness. Space is space for healing, wellness, for creating abundance, for the creation of whatever you desire, and for serving your life purpose.

Remember for a moment what I said about life force. Our life force is so often and easily wasted or compromised: by being in a boring conversation, by someone who is suppressing you or bothering or blaming you, or someone who is making you feel guilty.

Whenever you compromise yourself,
that's life force that is compromised.

The same life force that you could use to run a marathon, walk, drink more water, drink wheatgrass juice, prepare a vegan meal, go to the convenience store and get yourself the lottery ticket that wins you $365 million might be completely lost for suppressive purposes. It is the life force for the idea for the next great invention. It is the life force that you could utilize for writing the song that would make generations of music lovers tap their feet and hum along each time it is being played. Your life force and space itself are unlimited in potential.

What you do with that life force, and with the space in which you can unfold your life force is truly unlimited. You could strike a rock and have a spring come out of it. Or, you sit on the couch and nothing happens. Or you just go and take a shower. Either way it's the same life force and it has encapsulated in itself infinite and unlimited potential. In that space, you could create anything you wanted, you only need to decide to do so. See: How long does it take to go in the convenience store and get you that ticket? Maybe five minutes. That's five minutes of time and of space. How long does it take to come up with a great invention? Maybe just one minute. Then you write your idea down and you got it. That's the space that you have. That's the power of space. How and what you do with that space and how you fill it with your life force is up to you. That's why creating space is so important for yourself and for all of your clients: Creating space will remind us that we can start expanding our own life force so that we may live our full potential.

MODULE 5: ENTITIES, EARTHBOUND SPIRITS, EXTRATERRESTRIALS AND LETTING GO OF PARASITIC RELATIONSHIPS (THE EX)

Frequently, our life force is compromised due to attachments of heavy energies or entities that feed from it, and thereby deprive us of the full use of our life force. The following protocol addresses this situation:

"Any entities that are draining my life force in unhealthy ways, can you hear me?"

—The entities that are present will respond.

"Entities, please give me enough space so I can integrate more life force into my system."

"Entities, I give you now permission to start the transformational process, and please go into the greater central sun, into your own transformation."

It's a form of support.

When I declare, "Entities, I give you permission to start the transformational process and go into the greater central sun," I extend a form of support to these entities. The greater central sun is the mother of all the suns, and entities can find there their own healing transformation. They will be transformed into a raw energy form where they can start realizing their own full potential, rather than feeding on someone else. Most entities were not there to do us any harm. Some of them yes, but a lot of them came because we did not feel strong enough alone. So they came and kind of hang out with us, until we decide we're strong enough. It is sufficient to end this alliance by gently thanking them and pointing the way for them to a better place to be: "Thank you. I can handle this. Thank you for having been there. Now I give you permission to start the transformational process and go into the greater central sun for your own transformation."

The same applies to earthbound spirits:

"Any earthbound spirits draining my life force in an unhealthy way, can you hear me?"

The earth bound spirits say "Yes." Then we ask the earthbound spirits to start the transformational process by going into the greater central sun into their own transformation:

"Any earthbound spirits draining my life force in an unhealthy way, I give you permission to start the transformational process and go into the greater central sun."

Earthbound beings are stuck. They haven't gotten the news yet that they are dead. They are still going to work or doing their own little things, and don't know that they are dead. They are not conscious of their death, and are stuck, that's all. Sometimes when they are stuck, they can deal with you as if you were invading their space. If a spirit is still in a place where it thinks it still needs to work, and its workspace is not there anymore, it will create disturbances in one way or another. If it happens that you are living in that deceased person's house but you redesigned the house, or their workplace is now an apartment complex, then that person—that earthbound spirit—thinks you are invading their workplace.

That gives you an idea about what is occurring when you're walking into old battlefields from the Civil War, or into an Indian burial ground, or a place where tragic things had happened. Some of these beings who were alive then and part of a traumatic experience that led to their death can't get over the shock because it happened so fast that they didn't get the message. Without awareness of that, you might just be wondering why it feels so heavy to be in a specific place. Having awareness of what is truly going on, all you need to do is to give them an alternative to the experience in which they find themselves stuck. They will gladly take it! Once they move on from the place where they were stuck, they are given a chance to transform.

It is the same with extraterrestrial (ET) beings if they are affecting you.

You need to start by asking the ET beings that are attacking you to please give you more space. First of all you ask for more space because you might want to be a great host but you don't want to be drained. They are draining you in an unhealthy way. No one has the right to drain you. You have the right to your own space.

"Any extraterrestrial beings that are draining my life force, can you hear me?"

—The ET beings that are present will respond.

"Extraterrestrial beings that are draining my life force, I give you permission to go into the greater central sun, into your own transformation."

Next we address life-force that is still taken from us by ex-partners without our permission, i.e., during the separation or divorce process:

"All of my life-force that my ex is still taking from me without my permission, can you hear me?"

Once it answers with "Yes," we ask:

"All of my life-force that my ex is still taking from me without my permission, please fully return to me and stay with me."

Next, we say:

"All of my life-force that I still freely give to my ex, can you hear me?"

Once it answers with "Yes," we ask:

"All of my life-force that I still freely give to my ex, please fully return to me and stay with me."

In conclusion of this module, I wish to remind you that this is all about energy. No one has the right to drain you, and it is your right and duty to yourself to ask these beings to make space and leave you, and to start their own transformational process.

You might wonder why anyone could ever be draining another being since we—including the beings who might drain you—are all unlimited beings. We are indeed unlimited source beings. We are all connected to our unlimited source. Despite this fact, some beings choose to receive energy parasitically. In these situations, you need to take your power back, and let them know that you are asking for more space.

You have the right to your own space. You are compromised for some reason—in your own program or lineage program. Whatever the reason was, you now ask for your space ("Please give me more space"). That's when you can take a breath and develop greater consciousness and start really working on any given situation in your life that you wish to improve. Remember space is also connected to the unlimited vastness, when you ask for space it can be a little bit or a whole lot.

MODULE 6: BUILDING TRUST

The sixth module is to build trust when working with people who lost their trust in the universe or multiverse or in God or in themselves.

"My shattered trust in myself, the universe, God and humanity, can you hear me?"

Once we get an answer we ask, "My shattered trust in myself, the universe, God and into humanity, please start the healing process."

"My trust in myself, the universe, God and humanity, please become fully accessible and fully integrated into my life."

"Trusting in my purpose, can you hear me?"

Once we receive an answer, we ask, "Trusting in my purpose, please become fully present in my everyday life as well."

MODULE 7: CLEARING UP BLACK MAGIC

The following protocol assists you when you or your clients deal with psychic attacks, black magic, jealousy, spells, curses, dense energies, or Entities.

"Any jealousy projections that are affecting my energies in an unhealthy way, can you hear me?"

Once you receive an answer, say, "Please give me more space, start the transformational process and be deflected now."

In a next step you wish to clear yourself or your client from any form of black magic:

"Any form of black magic that is affecting me in an unhealthy way, can you hear me?"

Once you receive an answer, maybe in form of an energy response in the different areas of the body, say:

"Any form of black magic that is affecting me in an unhealthy way, please start the transformational process and give me more space."

This addresses anything that might have originated in this lifetime or in a past life since it is likely that people who engaged in black magic in a past life are experiencing repercussions in this life. If that might be the case, use the following protocol:

"Any black magic from my past lives, can you hear me?"

"Yes."

"Any black magic from my past lives, I now give you permission to start the transformational process and to be completely cleared."

When we don't have any black magic in our system, we don't attract black magic either.

When we approach the transformational aspect of these things, we have to consider our own relation to the subject in question. For instance: Have I attracted black magic in this life? Did I engage in black magic in a past life? It doesn't matter whether this relation is big or small, and whether it stems from a past or current life. We have to acknowledge and address it.

Note that this is a parallel process to what we had discussed with respect to entities: We attracted them and gave them permission to be with us, because it's like the saying has it, "misery loves company." If we are not miserable, we don't feel alone. We can then move forward. If we are busy moving forward, we will have no time to complain or to be burdened by another group of entities that don't want to move forward into the light.

Next, let's focus on the clearing of any dense energies:

"Any dense energies that are slowing me down, can you hear me?"

Once they answer, ask them to start the transformational process and give you more space:

"Any dense energies that are slowing me down, please start the transformational process and give me more space."

"Any dense energies that are making me feel heavy, can you hear me?"

Once they answer, ask them to start the transformational process and give you more space:

"Any dense energies that are making me feel heavy, please start the transformational process and give me more space."

"Any dense energies that are holding me back from seeing my light, can you hear me?"

Once they answer, ask them to start the transformational process and give you more space:

"Any dense energies that are holding me back from seeing my light, please start the transformational process and give me more space."

"Any dense energies that are holding me back from seeing my light, I now give you permission to be transformed and be replaced with my light."

Finally, focus on your psychic protection:

"My psychic protection, can you hear me?"

If the psychic protection says "Yes," then ask:

"My psychic protection, please become fully present in my everyday life."

MODULE 8: HOPELESSNESS AND HELPLESSNESS

Helplessness is the feeling that you can't do it—whatever "it" might represent—on your own. Hopelessness is the feeling that you don't want to live, or you feel like you cannot do anything any longer. When you or your clients feel hopeless and helpless, the following protocol will assist you to conduct the Sacred Inner Dialogue.

"My hopelessness, can you hear me?"

once it answers

"My hopelessness, please give me more space so I can fully connect to my life force."

"My hopelessness, please give me more space so I can fully connect with hope again."

"My helplessness, can you hear me? Once it answers, say:

Please give me more space so I can connect with the energy of successful solutions and support."

MODULE 9: SELF-LOVE AND SELF-WORTH

"My compromised self-love, can you hear me?"

Once it says, "Yes, I can hear you," then say: "My compromised self-love, please start the self-healing process."

Then we ask, "Self-love can you hear me?" —without the *compromised*! If your self-love says, "Yes, I can hear you," then say: "My self-love, please increase to the highest level possible."

If you or your client doesn't feel a response, you might still feel an energy. It is only the case in rare situations that we do not feel anything. If you or your client doesn't feel any energy, it means that you are a little too detached from your energy body or the aspect that you are addressing is non-existent. However, it is more typical to receive a "Yes" or "No." "Yes" and "No" are great answers. If the answer is a "Yes," that's ideal. If the answer is a "No," that means the aspect also heard it, but doesn't want to cooperate. When it answers "No," the aspect you were calling basically say's "I don't want to hear you," when it actually hears you because otherwise it wouldn't say "No."

If it says "No," then you say, "I know exactly that you heard me, otherwise you wouldn't say 'No.'"

Once it knows you can hear it, it has to answer you. You know why? Because you are the owner of your system. It is just a little program that runs in your system because you gave it permission and you are the owner of your system.

If you don't receive an answer when addressing self-love, then go back into compromised self-love.

Once you addressed compromised self-love, and it hears you and it starts the self-healing process, then move on to self-love,

"Self-love, can you hear me?"

It will now hear you because obviously you transformed the compromised self-love. Now that your self-love can respond here, ask:

"Self-love, please increase to the highest level possible."

Next, we are going to follow the same protocol with self-worth.

"My compromised self-worth, can you hear me?"

Once it answers with "Yes," say: "My compromised self-worth, please start the self-healing process."

Having addressed the compromised form of self-worth, we now address self-worth:

"My self-worth can you hear me?"

Once it answers with "Yes," say: "My self-worth, please increase to the highest level possible."

—Since your compromised self-worth has already started the self-healing process, your self-worth will increase to the highest level possible.

Observe the intensity of your self-worth and locate it on a scale from zero to ten, which marks the highest level possible. Observe where it is, then ask it to raise itself to level ten if it is not already there:

"My self-worth, please raise yourself to a level ten."

EXCURSUS: ASSESSMENT SYSTEM 0 - 10

Please apply this same assessment system to raise other aspects of your being, i.e., healing, prosperity, wellbeing, success, happiness, compassion and love.

The aspect that you address will start increasing and manifest itself in terms of self-appreciation and appreciation that you will receive from the world and from others.

MODULE 10: HEALTH

"My compromised health, can you hear me?"

Once it answers "Yes," please say:

"My compromised health, please start the self-healing process.

"My compromised immune system, can you hear me?"

Once it answers "Yes," please say:

"My compromised immune system, please start the self-healing process."

If we have something specific going on in our body, we can address this, i.e., we can address our compromised liver, our compromised gallbladder, or our compromised internal organs.

Follow this SID script:

"My compromised internal organs, can you hear me?"

Once they answer with "Yes," say:

"My compromised internal organs, I now give you permission to start the self-healing process."

We start our SID with addressing all compromised internal organs, and then we continue by zooming in to the exact organs and aspects that we wish to improve.

We ask our organs and aspects individually:

"My compromised liver, can you hear me?"

Once it answers with "Yes," ask:

"My compromised liver, please start the self-healing process."

"My compromised gallbladder, can you hear me?"

Once it answers with "Yes," ask:

"My compromised gallbladder, please start the self-healing process."

"My compromised heart, can you hear me?"

Once it answers with "Yes," ask:

"My compromised heart, please start the self-healing process."

"My compromised lungs, can you hear me?"

Once they answer with "Yes," ask:

"My compromised lungs, please start the self-healing process."

"My compromised kidneys, can you hear me?"

Once they answer with "Yes," ask:

"My compromised kidneys, please start the self-healing process."

"My compromised pancreas, can you hear me?"

Once it answers with "Yes," ask:

"My compromised pancreas, please start the self-healing process."

"My compromised brain, can you hear me?"

Once it answers with "Yes," ask:

"My compromised brain, please start the self-healing process."

"My compromised digestive system, can you hear me?"

Once it answers with "Yes," ask:

"My compromised digestive system, please start the self-healing process."

If there is anything in addition that you wish to address, please feel free to add it to this script.

We conclude by focusing on our compromised body and our compromised life:

"My compromised body, can you hear me?"

Once it answers with "Yes," ask:

"My compromised body, please start the self-healing process."

"My compromised life, can you hear me?"

Once it answers with "Yes," ask:

"My compromised life, please start the self-healing process."

MODULE 11: CANCER AND AUTOIMMUNE

This module deals with cancer and autoimmune diseases, which—whenever present—tend to cause major disruption and suffering. Although energetic shifts often occur instantaneously, be prepared to revisit these topics over a longer period, and to support your client or yourself in the self-healing process.

"Any form of cancer that is in my system, can you hear me?"

After a positive response, continue:

"Any form of cancer that is in my system, please start the transformational process."

"The cause for the cancer in my system, can you hear me?"

After a positive response, continue:

"The cause for the cancer in my system, start the expedited self-healing process."

Asking for the start of an expedited self-healing process, is a very important step in order to get ourselves or our clients back to life. This is possible as long as the person battling cancer is not in a necessarily terminal state, or has already made the decision to go.

Next, we ask the cause for the cancer in our past lives if it can hear us, and we ask it to start the transformational and expedited self-healing process. (Potentially life-threatening diseases can have very deep roots in our system from five years ago to life times ago, which could mean that we need to go one or more life times back to locate their origin. Luckily, this is something SID allows us to address effectively.)

"The cause for any cancer in my past life, can you hear me?"

After a response, continue:

"The cause for any cancer in my past life, start the transformational and expedited self-healing process." This goes also for chronic illnesses, allergies, viral/bacterial infections, genetic diseases, injuries, HIV/AIDS and other ailments.

EXCURSUS: WHY WE GET SICK

The following information is essential to understanding why we get sick, and by implication, this knowledge helps us to heal our bodies and our lives. The theory behind diseases is that we are creating these diseases so we can learn something from them.

If your clients or you yourself face specific issues, which can be real or a theory you hold, you as a practitioner and self-healer want to integrate that knowledge. If there is something you can learn from this disease, incorporate it into your identity. Sometimes disease slows us down, sometimes it makes us reach faster for our goals, it makes us wittier and shows us that we can overcome greater challenges than we had ever believed we could face, and be actually stronger than we thought we ever could be.

We are also co-creators of our reality. Everything we experience, we co-created. We are not helpless victims and life just happens to us. It is rather the case that we choose—even prior to our incarnation—that we will go through specific phases in our lives, so we grow from them.

Ultimately, all of our life experiences come down to choices. There's the 0.1% mystery from the divine, and nobody knows what's going to happen in that respect, but besides that, we have a huge chance to realize our function in the creation of patterns or diseases and to make successful adjustments. We can start transforming our harmful patterns and our diseases. For example, we know if someone smokes for fifty years, it can yield bad health consequences even though there are some smokers who live until they are one hundred and ten and they are okay. Either way, there's no "one size fits all" when it comes to the best individual life design. Still: Fact is, if you smoke less, you have a greater chance to live long and healthfully. I want us to take the responsibility of knowing that we are able to clarify and understand what our part is energetically in the process of co-creating our lives. Then, we can start transforming energetically any dense manifestation of a disease. To some extent it is true to say that we can't transform everything in our experience, however, some aspects we can improve greatly with a shift in emotional, mental, spiritual or physical attitude towards life.

Seeing our part in this and seeing how we can start transforming these patterns is essential and SID allows us to do exactly that. We can go immediately into seeing the cause of a disease and start asking if there's anything that needs to be done.

For instance, you might ask the cause of your acne to reveal itself to you, and get as a response—which can come to us in form of a sudden intuition or a feeling—that the cause for your acne is suppressed anger. You can ask then your suppressed anger what you can do for it, so that it will not need any longer to manifest in form of acne on your skin. The answer that comes to you might simply be to express anger respectfully and without harm to anyone else, so that it won't need to sit literally underneath your skin and cause breakouts.

It is a wise approach to check in with your immune system, liver, gallbladder, internal organs, entire physical body, limbs, bones, ligaments, muscles, skin, cells, DNA, energy and brain, emotional, mental body and your spiritual body, asking what you can do for it to optimize its workings.

MODULE 12: THE FIVE BODIES + TWO

The next part is intended for addressing anything in our mental, physical, emotional, spiritual and astral bodies.

"My mental body, can you hear me?"

"Yes."

"My mental body, please start the self-healing process in all areas of your being."

"My spiritual body, can you hear me?"

"Yes."

"My spiritual body, please start the self-healing process in all areas of your being."

"My emotional body, can you hear me?"

"Yes."

"My emotional body, please start the self-healing process in all areas of your being."

"My astral body, can you hear me?"

"Yes."

"My astral body, please start the self-healing process in all areas of your being."

"My physical body, can you hear me?"

"Yes."

"My physical body, please start the self-healing process in all areas of your being."

Most of us are fairly familiar with these five energy bodies. Besides them, there exist two more bodies: our pain body and our light body, which we both need to address for our full self-healing. Similar to the seven chakras, we have seven different bodies. We ask all these bodies to start the self-healing process on all levels.

"My pain body, can you hear me?"

"Yes."

"My pain body, please start the self-healing process on all levels."

People hold pain in their system. —Here's what's happening when we decide to talk to our pain body and ask it to start the self-healing process: It starts the self-healing process, not immediately super-fast, but it's like a detox that you put into motion, which builds up into a healthier environment that allows for healing. The next thing is a small healing crisis, which is perfectly normal. That crisis in itself is already an important sign of moving forward. Now we ask the following of the pain body, since it is still grounded in this existence:

"My pain body, please start the healing and ascension process."

We have one more body, we haven't considered, which is our light body. After the pain body, we have to work with the light body.

"My light body, can you hear me?"

"Yes."

"My light body, please start the self-healing process in all areas of your being, on all levels, and be activated now."

If we address all of our seven bodies, we achieved truly a full spectrum activation.

MODULE 13: LACK CONSCIOUSNESS & PROSPERITY PROGRAM

Before we can start addressing our lack consciousness and replacing it with a prosperity program, we need to start with self-love and self-worth (see Module 9). Once we ask self-love and self-worth if they can hear us and we receive a positive response, we ask them to raise themselves to their highest levels. After working on self-love and self-worth, we turn to generational lineage programming that is holding us back:

(A) First we support the lineage by addressing lack consciousness programming that is present in our lineage even though it might not directly affect us:

Ask: "Any lack consciousness programming in my lineage, can you hear me?"

Once it answers "Yes," say:

"Any lack consciousness programming in my lineage, please start the transformational process now."

(B) Next we address lack consciousness programming from our lineage that is also affecting us directly:

Ask: "The lack consciousness programming from my lineage that is also affecting me, can you hear me?"

Once it answers "Yes," say:

"The lack consciousness programming from my lineage that is also affecting me, please start the transformational process."

(C) Now we go into transforming any form of lack consciousness that is still holding us back:

Ask: "Any form of lack consciousness that's holding me back from living my full potential, can you hear me?"

Once it answers "Yes," say:

"Any form of lack consciousness that's holding me back from living my full potential, please start the transformational process."

Now address dysfunctional energies from your lineage that are also affecting you:

"Any dysfunctional energies from my lineage that are also affecting me, can you hear me?"

Once it answers "Yes," say:

"Any dysfunctional energies from my lineage that are also affecting me, please start the self-healing process."

(D) Now we work with our feeling of worthiness:

"My feeling of not being worthy, can you hear me?"

Once it answers "Yes," say:

"My feeling of not being worthy, please start the transformational process."

And we can add:

"My feeling of worthiness, can you hear me?"

Once it answers with "Yes," say:

"My feeling of worthiness, please raise yourself to the highest level possible."

Now address deserving the very best in life by saying:

"Deserving the very best in life, can you hear me?"

Once it answers with "Yes," say:

"Deserving the very best in life, please become fully present and reality now in all areas of my life, including my career."

(E) Then we go into balancing giving and receiving.

Most people who have lack consciousness feel that they are not getting enough and that they are giving too much. The sentiment is: "Whatever I do is never enough."

"The program of whatever I do is never enough, can you hear me?"

Once it answers "Yes," say:

"The program of whatever I do is never enough, please start the transformational process and be replaced with a healthier new program."

"The new program is, 'Everything I do is a miracle' and 'Everything I do is more than enough.'"

Then we turn to the balance of giving and receiving:

"My balance of giving and receiving, can you hear me?"

Once it answers "Yes," say:

"My balance of giving and receiving, please become fully present in my everyday life."

If I am in balance of giving and receiving,
I am perfectly prosperous.

(F) Next we turn to prosperity:

"My prosperity, can you hear me?"

Once it answers "Yes," say:

"My prosperity, please become fully present now and always in my life."

Now we continue by asking:

"All of my belief systems that are still supporting lack consciousness, can you hear me?"

Once it answers "Yes," say:

"All of my belief systems that are still supporting lack consciousness, I now give you permission to be transformed and replaced with a healthier new belief system."

"The new healthy belief system is: 'I now support prosperity in my life.'"

Now affirm:

"My new healthy belief system is: 'I now support prosperity in my life.'"

Continue by asking:

"My new healthy belief system 'I now support prosperity in my life,' can you hear me?"

Once it answers "Yes," say:

"My new healthy belief system 'I now support prosperity in my life,' be initialized and activated to support prosperity consciousness, prosperity belief systems, and prosperity experiences in all areas of my life."

I recall a session with a client who had a past life experience of being a French soldier in the Napoleonic War of 1812 in Russia, where he suffered from this immense sense of starvation when the Russian winter decimated large parts of Napoleon's army. He felt like he never had enough of anything. His experience could even be compared to living in France in the times leading up to the Revolution, descriptions of which you might recall from *Les Misérables* by Victor Hugo. People had such unbearable experiences of lack of nearly everything from food to clothes and firewood. Or a past life experience in a Nazi concentration camp, or a past life during the Great Depression. These can result in deeply ingrained programs of lack consciousness. These programs of lack consciousness generate a feeling of not being able to fully trust in life. The person who is affected by these programs will feel that he cannot trust life to provide for him, and therefore, he cannot trust any form of abundance and prosperity in his life. That's why it is important to address past lives and address any form of lack consciousness.

"Any lack consciousness from trauma in past lives in my system, can you hear me?"

Once it answers "Yes," say:

"Any lack consciousness from trauma in past lives in my system, please start the self-healing and transformational processes and give me more space so I can truly experience abundance in all areas of my life."

MODULE 14: ATTRACTING HEALTHY RELATIONSHIPS

"The higher self of my ideal life partner (soul mate, twin flame) can you hear me?"

Repeat out loud: "The higher self of my ideal life partner (soul mate, twin flame) can you hear me?"

If we get a response, then we say: "The higher self of my ideal life partner (soul mate, twin flame), please find me and become discoverable to me starting today."

EXCURSUS: INTUITIVE TESTING

It's important that you understand that Sacred Inner Dialogue can be used similar like muscle testing. You know how you can muscle test with kinesiology—when you ask the body a question and the body gives an answer, i.e. literally an answer in form of a physical response. In the same manner as muscle testing, there's a way that we can use SID as a tool for mental or emotional or spiritual testing. It can provide us with information, similarly to the information you receive through muscle testing. Sacred Inner Dialogue means basically that you ask a question related to the person and the person (it might be yourself or a client) becomes the channel for receiving an answer. You become literally a channel or a medium that makes your inner belief systems and energy patterns visible. This modality is so important because it truly empowers you to break through your limitations. Ultimately, you make a change because you started to address the issue, you began the dialogue with yourself. By you doing all of this by yourself, you have a full spectrum outcome instead of the experience of someone else doing the work for you. You raise your consciousness and become a better channel and medium every time you work with SID.

Ultimately, we all created our own reality. When we recognize that we are constantly engaged in creating our reality, we can consciously create and recreate, remodel and change at will what our reality looks like. That's when we are truly (re-)harnessing our power of creation. When we start communicating with SID and learn to be connected to our inner world and embrace who we are, we are re-emphasizing our power. We are re-emphasizing our co-creations because we created these patterns and everything else in our lives in the first place. That's what gives us the power to change them.

When we use SID, a lot of questions can be asked. For example, it's January, a person who is not employed and doesn't exactly know when the next employment will materialize, can simply ask, "Me starting my new work in June, can you hear me?" If the answer is a "No," she continues: "Me starting my new work in May, can you hear me?" Whenever there is no energetic response or even physical goosebumps or a mental image coming up, or emotionally, spiritually, or mentally at least a light response, then there is obviously no energy response to it, which is different from receiving a negative response, i.e., "No," which indicates a clear answer to the question "Yes or No?" This is not to be mixed up with the regular SID protocols in which you just want the issue addressed to make itself visible with an answer that the question went through and was heard. "Yes or No" are great because both are considered a positive response in SID, because it did respond.

You can move the date closer or further away to find out when your client will be employed again. This is similar to kinesiology, muscle testing.

With some clients you might get responses quicker, and with others the responses take a moment. When you go into the mental testing it is a good strategy to zoom in. For instance, if there was a positive response to the question, "Me starting my new work in May, can you hear me?" and you are now asking, "Me starting my new work at the 25th of May" and your client does not get another positive response, I would expand it back into April. Next I instruct my client to ask, "Me starting my new work in early May or end of April, can you hear me?" until we get a response. Once we get a response, we can start narrowing it down: "Me starting my new work by the 10th of April, can you hear me?" If no positive response, continue asking:

"Me starting my new work by the 5th of April, can you hear me?" and suddenly your client feels an energy sensation! It gets a little bit warmer, so we continue our fine-tuning: "Me starting my new work by the 3rd of April, can you hear me?" If the client starts feeling a tingling sensation in her body and the feeling gets stronger, then that's a pretty strong response already. It means there's already a lot of great feedback. Observe also your own energy responses as a cross-reference. Since we as practitioners are usually empaths, we can fairly easily resonate with the feelings of our clients, which allows us to accompany and guide them in their process. Now we are going further into determining the exact date. We instruct our client to say: "Me starting my new work on the 1st or 2nd of April, can you hear me?" and now the energy gets stronger and nears its peak. We ask our client to inquire one more time: "Me starting my new work at the 2nd of April, can you hear me?" and then the energy response is not as strong. Then I ask her to affirm: "Me starting my new work on April 1st, can you hear me?" and that generates an energy response so powerful, far more powerful than the prior responses, so then I know this is likely the date by which she is going to start her new work. April Fool's Day, interesting date but so be it.

There are no limitations with respect to the topics to which you can apply SID. It is a very powerful intuitive tool that gives us great possibilities to work with information on our energetic physical, emotional, mental and spiritual wellbeing.

Ultimately, remember that Sacred Inner Dialogue is not so much there to diagnose, but to support your system energetically.

MODULE 15: CHAKRA ASSESSMENT

For a chakra assessment, we start with the first chakra, and we follow the script as described here:

"My first chakra, can you hear me?"

Once it answers with "Yes," we can go further.

We can ask:

"My first chakra, is there anything I can do for you?"

That question will reveal important information to you. Following that step, you can ask your first chakra to optimize its workings:

"My first chakra, please spin at the highest frequency possible."

You can also decide to support all chakras at once:

"All of my chakras, please spin at the highest frequency possible."

Ideally, you spend a little time to address each chakra separately and to assess it ("What can I do for you?). Conclude each time by asking the respective chakra to spin at the highest frequency possible.

If you have some chakras that don't want to spin right away when you ask them to do so, you know that the organs and glands related to that chakra also play a role in the way the chakra reacts to SID since that chakra serves us as an energizer for these organs. In these cases, there might be a physical imbalance that needs to be addressed.

Here are some key correlations between chakras and organs and glands, as well as key phrases that can be used to activate each chakra:

1st / root chakra "I have"	male/female reproductive organs, testes, kidneys, spine, reproductive glands
2nd / sacral chakra "I feel"	bladder, prostate, ovaries, kidneys, gall bladder, bowel, spleen, adrenal glands; regulates immune system and metabolism
3rd / solar plexus "I can"	gall bladder, intestines, pancreas, liver, bladder, stomach, upper spine; regulates metabolism
4th / heart chakra "I love"	breasts, heart, lungs, thymus gland; regulates the immune system
5th / throat chakra "I communicate"	bronchial tubes, vocal chords, respiratory system, all areas of the mouth, including tongue and esophagus; thyroid gland; regulates body temperature and metabolism
6th / third eye chakra "I see"	eyes, brain, pineal and pituitary glands; produces hormones and governs the function of the previous glands
7th / crown chakra "I know"	spinal cord and brainstem, pineal gland; regulates biological cycles, including sleep

For more information on chakras, please visit my website www.ataanamethod.com

Each chakra has also a phrase that allows you to directly call upon and energize that chakra. For instance, if a person indicates a problem with the third chakra, our assessment of the chakra will likely show a compromised situation in that person's life relating to the "I can" - statement. At the same time, using these statements can not only reveal stuck energy or some kind of issue related to that chakra, but also—when used as affirmations—help to overcome such compromised situation.

Below are the phrases that go with each chakra. I decided to list the chakras here with their original, Sanskrit names, starting from the first chakra and ending with the Aura:

Muladhara — I have

Svadhisthana — I feel

Manipura — I can

Anahata — I love

Vishuddha — I communicate

Ajna — I see

Sahasrara — I know

Aura — I am

Let's say you or your client faces blockages in the third chakra, you can work with the corresponding phrase: "Manipura, I can!"

A blockage indicates what the person believes, or rather doesn't believe. Someone with problems in the third chakra, does not believe that she can do whatever it is she has to do in her life (whatever her purpose might be). The moment I—as a practitioner—find out about this through SID, I can immediately work with the third chakra.

A person who has a blockage in the first chakra, has a problem with owning, even with owning up to something. This concerns all aspects of having as well: having time, having space, having money, having land, having a home, having anything goes with that. As a practitioner, I would be made aware of this, when there is no response, no energy whatsoever in response to the basic question: "First chakra, can you hear me?"

It is important to know that whenever one chakra is not working properly, the others are nearly always out of balance as well, and need therefore appropriate support.

So, what can I do when I detect a blockage in any of the chakras?

Let's stick with the example of the first chakra. The Sacred Inner Dialogue would evolve like this:

MULADHARA — I HAVE

Please look also up Module 3: GROUNDING.

"First chakra, can you hear me?"

—No response.

I would then ask my first chakra (or encourage my client to ask his first chakra):

"Is there anything I can do for you?"

If there's still no response, we ask:

"Anything blocking the first chakra, can you hear me?"

Once we get a response, we say:

"Anything blocking my first chakra, please give me more space and start the transformational process."

I repeat this, until there is enough space so that the chakra can start to answer. Once that chakra starts to answer, that's when we can start working with it. Then we can use the phrase that goes with that chakra in order to energize it ("Muladhara, I have!").

The blockage in the chakra is most often caused by a belief. For instance, with respect to the first chakra: Whatever it is, a person believes she doesn't have is of course exactly what she does not have. This belief, if left unchecked in the system, is bound to manifest its physical equivalent. (In the same manner, it holds true: Whatever someone believes to have, sooner or later, she is going to have it.) If you can keep an uninterrupted thought internally and externally alive for a certain amount of time, then the reality is that it has to materialize in some way or form. That's great, if it is in the highest interest for everyone involved. If the thought is of a low frequency though, unfortunately, it can materialize too and can cause much harm. In consolation: a low frequency thought materializes slower and with more effort than a high frequency thought. If the thought is a wish that's not interfering with the rest of the world, or if it's a big thought that is in alignment with your Self and with creation, the Multiverse will look into creating it and bringing it to you swiftly.

In this instance, with the first chakra, I could now go into the sex organs, the lower back, and into grounding, which are all tied together in the first chakra. I could work on mother issues, I could work on grounding, and on the earth connection. All of these have to be considered and worked on in order to get good results. More than anything, it is important to get to a place of having, of knowing, and of trusting Mother Earth that we're part of this planet and we have our proper space.

We could even go into the organs for deeper self-healing, and into the legs, the femur, the knees—everything that is in the first chakra, everything that it stands for. That's the full spectrum approach.

Being able to do so through Sacred Inner Dialogue is greatly different, and in a way more direct and efficient in leading to a harmonious solution, from merely addressing the same issue psychologically. The full spectrum approach allows me to recognize that a "mother issue"—to stick with our example here—is also a Mother Earth issue and a female energy issue, and we further know that in that case, we need to balance the male/female energy in the person as well. This gives people a chance to start transforming things on a whole other level.

It gives us opportunities to access and support the body in an advanced manner without feeling that we are disconnected. It's one solution that can be applied anytime. Once you mastered this tool to bring about solutions to a situation, you can use this same tool over and over, and it becomes easier and easier for you to do so.

Next, we move up to the second chakra, and then upward to the remaining chakras until all chakras are properly addressed and cleared.

SVADHISTHANA — I FEEL

I ask: "My second chakra, can you hear me?" and that chakra says, "Yes."

At this point, I can even decide to assess the exact level at which this chakra works at that moment. I can ask: "My second chakra, what is your current frequency?" and add for clarification: "High is 10 and low is 0." If there is no immediate clear response, I ask further: "My second chakra, is your level 2 or above?" "Is it a 2?" "Is it a 3?" I could even start my asking at zero, which is extremely unlikely, but it could be so low so that I would want to ask: "Is your frequency a zero?" If there is no response, I move on: "Is it a 1?" Maybe I sense now that some energy is building up and it is getting a little warmer. From here, I'd go on: "Is your frequency a 2?" or "Is your frequency a 3?" When I come to 5, the chakra gives me a signal. I continue and ask: "Is your frequency a 6"—then it gets cold, and I know that the frequency of the chakra is at a 5 at this moment.

In a next step, I ask the chakra to optimize its working:

"My second chakra, please raise your frequency to a level 10."

Even though my chakra had not been at a 10 to begin with, I know now at least that it had been compromised, and I can immediately adjust my chakra and ask it to rise to a 10.

Ultimately, I do not only want to know where it is but ask it also, "Why was your frequency on 5 instead of 10?"—This is when the chakra will reveal information that I can then utilize for self-healing, and of course the same holds true if it is not my chakra but I am going with a client through that process. I might learn: "Oh, it's that low because the chakra was affected by abuse from childhood." Then I can go into the abuse in the childhood and ask the trauma from the abuse in childhood to start the healing process.

We are our own barometer. We can fully gauge what's going on with ourselves. That's the mechanism. SID is our tool because it helps us to get there.

MANIPURA — I CAN

We can approach our Manipura as we approached the other chakras, or we can simplify the script.

"My Manipura, can you hear me?"

Once it answers with "Yes," we ask our Manipura to spin at the highest level possible and start the self-healing process:

"My Manipura, please spin at the highest level possible and start the self-healing process."

ANAHATA — I LOVE

We can do the same with the heart chakra. We can ask: "At which frequency are you spinning—from a 10 high to a zero low?" The chakra might answer immediately: "I'm on a 3 or 4." This process does not need to be long or painstakingly; the chakra will give you right away the information if possible, which is dependent on how connected a person is with her own inner self. If you encounter a client who does not appear to have a strong connection so that SID would yield prompt reactions, do instead of Sacred Inner Dialogue energy work on that person. Some people are responding better to energy work, some people are responding better to SID and some people are responding perfectly to both. These are truly tuned-in people. The more they are tuned-in to their inner selves, the faster they can change and can attract major breakthroughs.

If the heart answers: "I am at a level 4," we can ask: "Why aren't you spinning at a 10?" It might say: "Because I'm still having pain in my heart from a recent break-up." Then we say to the pain in the heart: "Pain in my heart, can you hear me?"

Then we ask the pain in the heart to start the transformational healing process:

"Pain in my heart, please start the transformational healing process."

Then we can ask the heart to start the self-healing process.

"My heart, please start the self-healing process."

Then we can ask the heart chakra: "Please raise your frequency to a ten because there's nothing to hold you back." Ultimately, we have a right to be at a ten with our life's presence, so this is an important and justified demand.

VISHUDDHA — I COMMUNICATE

The same approach can be used with the fifth chakra: You would speak: "My fifth chakra, can you hear me?"

Once we receive a positive answer, ask: "At which frequency are you spinning?"

You might receive the response: "I'm spinning at a 7."

So, you would ask: "What needs to happen for you to spin at a 10?"

Your Vishuddha might explain to you: "I need to be allowed to communicate my truth because I was not allowed to do so in the past."

Then we ask: "Giving myself permission to communicate my truth, can you hear me?"

Once it answers "Yes," we say: "Giving myself permission to communicate my truth, please become my reality now."

Then we ask the Vishuddha:

"My Vishuddha, can you initiate the self-healing process?"

—Once it answers affirmatively, then we ask:

"My Vishuddha, please initiate the self-healing process now."

For bringing our Vishuddha to spin at a level 10, we ask:

"My Vishuddha, please raise your frequency to a ten and spin at the highest level possible."

AJNA — I SEE

The same applies to the sixth chakra, the third eye, the Ajna. Here is a guideline for a possible dialogue:

Say: "Ajna, can you hear me?"

Once it answers "Yes," ask:

"At what level from 0 to 10 are you spinning?"

The Ajna might answer:

"At a 3 or 4."

Then ask:

"Why, Ajna? Why aren't you spinning at a 9 or 10? What is holding you back? What is compromising you?"

The sixth chakra might say: "It's a past life."—Or it might reveal that there is something else that's blocking or clogging the third eye. In that case, you'd like to ask the past life experience or whatever is clogging the third eye to please be transformed and released so the third eye can spin at its highest level. Whatever disturbing image there might be, or whatever might be blocking the third eye, ask it to start the transformational process and ask it to be completely released. Then ask the Ajna to spin at a 10, the highest level possible:

"Ajna, please spin at a 10, at the highest level possible."

The mere act of going to a 10, the highest level possible, gives the chakra a better spin and improves seeing. This can also be done whenever we might not receive a clear answer from the Ajna or from any of the other chakras.

Note:

As the phrase that I shared above, "Ajna, I see!" indicates, the third eye has to do with seeing. Starting from the phrase that corresponds to the chakra on which you want to work, you could also initiate the dialogue by asking: "Ajna, what is it that you don't want to see or what is it that you saw?"

SAHASRARA — I KNOW

Please look also up the deeper explanation of this chakra under Module 4: CROWN CHAKRA.

We approach our Sahasrara by using either the following simplified SID-script, or by expanding this script with specific questions that allow us best to zoom in to our needs (or our client's needs) with respect to "knowing" in our lives.

"My Sahasrara, can you hear me?

Once it answers with "Yes," we ask our Sahasrara to spin at the highest level possible and start the self-healing process:

"My Sahasrara, please spin at a 10, the highest level possible and start the self-healing process."

AURA — I AM

We approach our Aura, our entire energy field in its totality, also by using either the following simplified SID-script, or by expanding this script with specific questions that allow us best to zoom in to our needs (or our client's needs) with respect to "being" in our lives.

"My Aura, can you hear me?

Once it answers with "Yes," we ask our Aura to raise itself to a level 10 and start the self-healing process:

"My Aura, please raise yourself to a level 10, the highest level possible, and start the self-healing process."

> *The Sacred Inner Dialogue is the*
> *first step toward healing.*

EXCURSUS: UNDERSTANDING OUR ROLE AS ENERGY HEALERS AND THE NECESSITY OF SELF-RECOGNITION

If you work with the third eye, you would typically want to leave it open so that you or your client can get a better insight and answer questions that come up in daily life in a better way. Teaching your client Sacred Inner Dialogue as described allows them also to initiate their own dialogues, to ask themselves in the future, and if they get an answer and can solve issues by themselves, then you have less to interfere with their inner processes and they benefit even more since you can utilize these new revelations for progress and you have more fun since its really moving forward. The more they come up with their own epiphanies, the more value their transformational work has, and the further they come in life's transformation in general. The more we become an assistant of the Creator with this process, the more we all benefit. For you as a practitioner, it is essential to guide your clients to a point where they do the work themselves, so that they can really undergo transformation. Having your clients do the work themselves, allows you also to go deeper into your self-healing.

That's how people get their power back.

They reach a place where they are able to say: "I am ready to transform this. I am ready to look at this. I'm ready to take my power back. I am ready to take responsibility." That's how a person benefits the most. (Of course, this means also for the healers, for you as a practitioner, not to strive to be the miracle magic healer, and say, "Oh look, I just did a gesture with my hands and the thing is transformed.")

Such miracle healing wouldn't help that person because that person created the stagnation in their system in the first place. If that person doesn't know—or learn—how to transform that stagnation, that stagnation can come back and that person can't fix it alone.

It is important to teach and empower your client in a healthy way. Ultimately, we have not yet reached our full potential as energy healers until we are facilitating the self-healing of a client in a way where it's happening by itself, by us merely providing the space. It's almost like a spa where the person reaches through relaxation the levels and depths of a problem and then starts transforming it with help of their higher selves. As energy healers, our role is in that situation to activate all the healing abilities and qualities of our client. We support our client in developing their self-healing abilities so that that person starts the self-healing process. The first step of this process is, obviously, to make that—any—stagnation visible.

It's like the immune system that doesn't even know that it's being compromised. Once you make it visible to the immune system, it starts to recognize what is wrong with itself. That's comparable to a urine therapy, where patients drink a few drops of their own urine in a glass of water to reflect homeopathically back to themselves and to their system whatever is in their system. Their system starts to recognize what's wrong in the system. Your system starts the self-healing process just by doing that. Just by raising awareness. This works because you are reflecting back to your system something of which your system doesn't have any idea since it had gotten so used to it that it became literally blind to it.

We have these perfect, unbelievably amazing systems in our bodies that can basically create anything. So once we know what it is exactly that we want to transform, we will start creating the antidote for it.

A more common example of the very same process is how we react to food. If you eat some types of food, our body—like a perfect alchemist—finds the exact enzymes to breaking down the food. Our body produces these enzymes. Producing these enzymes requires immense energy from the body. That's basically what your body has to do each time you eat cooked food. Let's say you eat a cooked potato, your body finds the exact enzyme that's breaking down that potato. Everything that you have cooked as well as any type of processed food, require immense effort from your body to produce the enzymes needed for digesting your food. However, let's say you've eaten a piece of fish or raw kale, or spinach. As long as it is raw, it has its own enzymes and our system does not need to produce enzymes to digest it.

Once your body starts breaking down food, i.e. digesting it, you can start getting the energy from it. That's why it's beneficial to eat raw food, preferably raw vegan food.

When you look into nature, you will see that animals wait a little after they killed their prey. During that time, the enzymes of the killed prey start to work. It is a rule in nature: If you leave a *natural* potential source of food untouched, it starts dissolving by itself. If you give it some time, it is going to dissolve. It has its own enzymes that carry their own program to dissolve it, to neutralize it, so-to-speak.

That's why it's important to have enzyme rich foods because it helps us to contain rather than waste our own enzymes. The more enzymes we have, the more life force we have because we don't have to produce these enzymes just to use them up again.

If you eat processed food, the energy needed to break it down is even more than what is needed for breaking down *natural* but cooked food. Think about it: First of all, you pay for that food, then you eat it, then your body has to make enzymes, and you pay on top of what you already paid in money now in form of energy that you need to spend, and only then you finally have your food as nourishment. In contrast, if you get something that is raw, you pay once for it and eat it, that's it. With cooked and processed food, you pay twice or even three times. With raw food, you just buy it and it's just yours.

Our systems are designed to function, heal and thrive.

Once we recognize this, we can start very easily our system's self-healing process. It's working for us, so we naturally work with it and do not resist it. Every time we cater toward this feeling, it will immediately access it. There might be a learning curve, similar to when people who used to smoke stop smoking, and then, after a while, they almost feel like throwing up if they have a cigarette. At that point, their system had already begun the clearing process. The period needed to clear up their system depends how much they taught themselves not to be healthy. Any system will naturally start to go toward health and harmony.

When you are a smoker, for example, you smoke and feel really good when you are having a cigarette even though in reality you should be throwing up because you just pumped tar in your system. Your system is totally overwhelmed. You stamped down your system with so much force, that it doesn't recognize any longer a toxin. Your body doesn't know anymore that cigarette smoke isn't good for you because you introduced that into your body every day for a prolonged period, and out of self-protection, the body found finally a way around it and said, "Okay, we're just going to accept it and store the toxins, i.e., in a protective fatty tissue, as not to overwhelm our system."

It is exactly the same with toxic thoughts and toxic habits that are introduced into your system. Your Self says after awhile, "Okay, we probably just have to get used to it and live with it." We manipulated our systems to accept toxic environments, toxic experiences, toxic moments, toxic habits. We don't even know that we have them in our minds and in our hearts or in our physical bodies. When we give our system a checkup, basically mirroring back to our system what is inside, the reaction of our system is like: "Whoa, what just happened?" We have to clear ourselves of these toxic energies, thoughts, entities or habits (addictions).

If you are a smoker and start on a detox program, you are going to feel really bad. If you do a footbath as a smoker or a heavy metal detox as a heavy smoker, you are probably not going to feel good. People call this a healing crisis. On the other hand, if you do a heavy metal detox, and you are not a smoker and have few toxins in your system, your body is not going to respond much to it.

A lot of times when people go into energy work, or SID, they may have a stronger response than expected because they have more toxicity in their system than they thought they had, where they were not even aware of their toxicity. Emotional toxins. Mental toxins. Spiritual toxins. Physical toxins. Then, once you start the clearing process, it becomes visible where you are at on the scale.

If you are a smoker and stop smoking, the first couple of weeks you are going to feel almost nauseated if you just take a deep breath of air while you should feel happy and be jumping for joy about the fresh air. Instead, you feel nauseated or like throwing up. Why? Because your system was used to the toxic smoke and you have to first undergo a healing crisis that makes you experience the healthy initially as what your system seems to reject. After a while, your system cleanses itself sufficiently and overcomes that stage.

With this illustration of how detoxing works, I don't want to criticize smokers. In the past, I was a smoker myself. It's more about understanding toxicity, understanding what toxins do to our system and understanding how our system responds to cleansing.

*Sacred Inner Dialogue is a cleansing
process that works on all levels.*

MODULE 16: TOXINS

Having learned in the preceding passage about toxicity and the effects of cleansing, I share here a SID protocol for detoxing our systems. You declare:

"All of the toxins that are in my system, can you hear me?

Once they answer with "Yes," say:

"All of the toxins that are in my system, I now give you permission to be released from my system in a healthy, graceful and loving way."

This means we are not overwhelming our system. We are not dumping all of our toxins into our bloodstream at once, as could happen on a physical level when you carry a lot of toxins and you decide to get fresh beet juice and your system starts detoxing rapidly, and you are saying, "Oh my goodness, what just happened?"

Something similar happens with wheat grass juice. If you start drinking two ounces of wheatgrass juice, it's like, "Whoa. That's bitter and then a little bit sweet." Do this every day and after a couple weeks or months, maybe you can try four ounces. Then you say, that's a whole lot, that's a lot of wheatgrass. Ultimately, wheat grass has everything that you need—proteins, amino acids, vitamins, it's basically the liquid green blood. It has everything to refresh the blood. If you then go after seven eight weeks up to six ounces to eight ounces, that's the time when you can measure your success and fully assess the condition of your system: "Unbelievable! I can handle eight ounces of wheatgrass? I am definitely in a detoxing process and I'm almost through with it."

If you do a juice fast for a month, you know your system is pretty clear if you make it through it, and still feel good a month after ending your fast. If you can do another juice fast after a month and a half, you obviously cleared something out. However, if you have some fresh organic juice every day, you will be able to maintain a consistently high level of health and energy effortlessly.

If you start in a rather radical manner with extremely healthy habits, you might create a drastic, intense response in your system that might be overwhelming. That's why you want to gently work on your system. Do it with grace. Expressing your intention in a graceful and loving way and acting accordingly is the best.

It's the same with Sacred Inner Dialogue:

When you work with SID, it causes
a very deep cleansing process.

To cleanse major aspects of your life, proceed in small increments and repeat the process frequently.

SID causes a cleansing process because we are going into deep core patterns of a person's life and we ask these patterns to shift. That's a big deal. These patterns were in place for a long time, maybe lifetimes, and all of a sudden they shift. The shifting of these patterns can lead them very fast to a point close to Enlightenment. It can also create a temporary healing crisis.

The shifting of these patterns can get them to a place of excellence. It can get them to a place of full functioning Oneness-consciousness.

Even if they get glimpses, it's a really good start for their system to remember all of that. That's why SID is so important. SID is exploring the inner worlds and outer worlds and enables people to really take their power back.

Here are some suitable SID scripts for detoxing:

"Any toxic thoughts and parasites in my system, I now give you permission to be lovingly and respectfully transformed and released and then replaced with healthier thoughts and healthier programs."

"My toxic emotions, can you hear me?"

Once they answer with "Yes," we tell them to start the transformational process:

"My toxic emotions, I now give you permission to start the transformational process."

"My toxic spiritual programming, can you hear me?

Once it answers with "Yes," we say to our toxic spiritual programming:

"My toxic spiritual programming, I now give you permission to start the transformational process and be replaced with a healthier program that fully supports my spiritual awakening."

We now address the physical toxins and parasites that are in our systems:

"Any physical toxins and parasites that are in my system, can you hear me?"

Once they answer with "Yes," we say:

"Any physical toxins and parasites that are in my system, I now give you permission to be released in a loving and respectful way and without any damage to my system."

—In this way, we're allowing these toxins to be released but in a loving and respectful way that does not hurt our system. Drinking enough water and sweating by working out, are ways in which we can support ourselves throughout that process.

Detox principles go as far as the parasites in the colon, we are asking them to lovingly and respectfully give us more space and to be transformed and released. That by its own can be so powerful that they start the transformational process and leave.

Toxic thoughts and habits that are still holding us back have to be considered as well.

"Any toxic habits in my system, can you hear me?"

Once they answer with "Yes," we say:

"I now give all of my toxic habits permission to be transformed, released and to be replaced with healthier habits, with habits that are life affirming".!!!!!!

Well Done!!!!!!!!!!

Good work, you truly are moving forward and clearing your life.!

14. AFFIRMATIONS

I wish to leave you with some SID approaches and affirmations:

Self-LAW: A quick, smart, short word for all these three: self-love, self-appreciation, self-worth.

I now increase my self-love, -appreciation and -worth

I now increase my self-LAW. When I increase my self-LAW, I increase my self-love, my self-appreciation and self-worth.

I now increase my self-worth and move fearlessly into my purpose.

From now on, I see myself in the highest light.

Instead of settling for less I choose success.

I am pre-approved. Today I am fully approving of myself. I am fully approved.

 I now activate my psychic protection.

The less I work, the more I earn.

There is clarity in my prosperity.

Ideas for SID approach:

Love can you hear me?

Healing can you hear me?

Clarity can you hear me?

Happiness can you hear me?

My new House for the right price at the right place can you hear me?

My strength can you hear me?

My light can you hear me?

The energy of Forgiveness can you hear me?

My psychic abilities can you hear me?

My purpose in life can you hear me?

My enlightenment can you hear me?

Pick one, then ask: Please become fully present in my everyday life.

15. IN CONCLUSION

I wish you success with applying SID in your personal and professional life. It has helped myself and many, many people with whom I have worked and continues to be one of my go-to tools on a daily basis. This is why I have shared this magnificent tool with you. Please respect it and approach it with humbleness. It will teach you so much about the richness of life and support you in your overall process of becoming whole again.

See you soon, traveler!

*Dedicated to the Creative source we all
come from and we all return to.*

*Thank you Tammy Badilli, Kathrin Seidl,
Sadiqua Hamdan, and Hannah Coleman.*

*Thank you to all the Angels that are
constantly supporting my work.*

Disclaimer

Self-healing is your own choice

*In the event of a medical emergency,
call a doctor or 911 immediately.*

*This book is designed to provide information to
my readers. No Healing warranties or guarantees
are expressed or implied by the Author. The author
shall not be liable for any physical, psychological,
emotional, spiritual, financial, or commercial
damages, including, but not limited to special,
incidental, consequential or other damages. Reading
this book is your own choice and at your own risk.*

*It is sold with the understanding that the
Author is not engaged to render any type of
medical, psychological, legal, or other advice.*

*This book is not intended to serve as a substitute for
the consultation, diagnosis, and/or medical treatment
of a qualified physician or healthcare provider.*

*Use sound Judgment and be the
best you can be at all times.*